Aron
Abra

Out of the

Archives

EARTH CHANGES
and
Much More

OZARK
MOUNTAIN
PUBLISHING

PO Box 754, Huntsville, AR 72740
479-738-2348 or 800-935-0045; fax 479-738-2448
www.ozarkmt.com

For permission, serialization, condensation, adaptions, or for our catalog of other publications, write to Ozark Mountain Publishing, Inc., P.O. box 754, Huntsville, AR 72740, ATTN: Permissions Department.

Library of Congress Cataloging-in-Publication Data
Abrahamsen, Aron, 1921- , Abrahamsen, Doris - 1926
    Out of the Archives, by Aron and Doris
Information from readings from the Akashic Records by Aron and Doris and includes predictions of earth changes to come.

1. Akashic Records   2. Earth Changes   3. Guides   4. Guardian Angels
I. Abrahamsen, Aron, 1921   II. Abrahamsen, Doris, 1926   III. Metaphysics
IV. Akashic Records

Library of Congress Catalog Card Number: 2011921733

ISBN: 978-1-886940-13-0

Cover Art and Layout: www.enki3d.com
Book set in: Times New Roman, Benquiat Bk BT
Book Design: Julia Degan

Published by:

OZARK
MOUNTAIN
PUBLISHING

PO Box 754
Huntsville, AR 72740
WWW.OZARKMT.COM
Printed in the United States of America

Table of Contents

Chapter 1

A Gift Discovered

L ittle did I realize when I came home from work that night in the spring of 1969 how the phenomenon that occurred during the next few minutes would change my life and alter my destiny.

It was my first out-of-body experience, and my life has never again been the same.

When my wife Doris and I started on our conscious search for God in 1953, neither of us had heard of out-of-body experiences or the Akashic records, and we were not even vaguely familiar with the concepts of reincarnation and karma. Please understand that in our fundamental Christian philosophy, there was simply no room for the notion of past lives and astral projection.

In time we found ourselves living in an intellectual religious utopia, and because of years of studying the scriptures, we thought we knew all the counsel and plan of God. It was the most remote thing from my mind that some day I would be going to the Akashic records and giving psychic readings.

Yet today we believe that this experience uprooted us out of our "paradise", and God used it as a new plow to break the fallow ground of our understanding of His ways and His love.

In the early 1960's, I began working for TRW (Thompson, Ramo, Woolridge, a multifaceted company.) I was assigned to the Minuteman Program Office, to work with the Minuteman ballistic missiles. We lived in Redlands, California, on the edge of an orange grove. Besides my demanding professional commitments, I often spoke to church groups on spiritual matters. We were very active in the charismatic movement. I also lectured to business groups and schools about the Apollo Space program, on which I worked in the early stages of its development.

During the course of my talks, sometimes I would feel an urgency to focus my attention toward an individual in the audience. I would stop what I was saying and convey the information that came to me for that person. Then I would continue my talk where I left off.

After these meetings, often the recipients of the messages would express their gratitude for what had been given because the information provided solutions to dilemmas that were troubling them.

This happened so frequently that word spread that I could get messages from God for those who were seeking guidance for their problems and situations. We began receiving letters and phone calls from desperate people who were in difficult circumstances and wanting advice.

To obtain the help they needed, I would quiet myself and begin to pray for them. To the best of my recollection, there was always an answer.

One particular evening when I had come home from a hectic day at TRW, I was tired, irritable and hungry. The only thing on my mind was dinner followed by rest and relaxation—but Doris had other ideas.

Earlier in the day, a letter had arrived from a young man who needed guidance on a decision about a matter of choosing between several job offers. He didn't know which one to take, so he asked for advice. Though we had never met, I supposed he had heard me speak somewhere, or he may have heard from others that I could get a message from God.

In any case, Doris believed his letter had a sense of urgency, and it deserved an answer at once. She suggested I pray for an answer while she finished preparing dinner. I objected, saying it could wait until after dinner, but Doris persisted.

So I sat down in my favorite rocking chair, took a deep breath, and relaxed. As I quieted myself and started to pray for this young man, something dramatically different happened.

Immediately, I was out of my body and on top the roof of my home. Looking around, I saw the tall eucalyptus trees a few hundred feet away, the orange grove directly behind me and to my right and left the three other homes in the cul de sac where we lived. I looked down through the rafters and saw myself sitting in the rocking chair in my living room. I remember thinking that it was interesting being in two places at once.

However, I sensed there must be a reason for being out of my body, so I pushed off the roof and flew up, soaring, and continuing to pray for that young man. Soon I found myself walking along a narrow path that was barely wide enough for one person. The path and the surrounding area were like soft, white billowing clouds.

It was extremely still, like after a snowfall when nature is covered with a gentle hush. Walking in solitude, I was filled with reverence for God as the sacred silence permeated my being.

As I walked along, I knew that somehow I was on my way to get information which might help that young man. Although this was a unique and unfamiliar experience for me, I had no fear or apprehension. Everything felt comfortable as if I knew exactly what I was doing. Coming to a fork in the path, I intuitively bore to the left then veered slightly to the right around the bend.

Stopping, I gazed upon a Grecian, temple-like palace with eight large columns supporting the roof. The entire structure was fashioned from pure white marble. Though I had never seen it before, it looked familiar. I understood at once that this was the place where the chronicles of each person's lives are recorded—the Akashic records.

The temple towered high above me, disappearing into the cloudbanks. As I was still far off, I longed to be there. Instantly, I found myself standing in front of the vast, marble platform where the Grecian columns reached skyward.

The platform of the temple was about two feet above the level where I was standing. I knew I had to get inside of the building to retrieve the information I was seeking. I stepped onto the platform. As I did, two men dressed in white togas appeared and welcomed me. One declared that they had been waiting for me, and that they were my guides. I told them about the young man's dilemma. They suggested that, perhaps, something from his past lives could give a clue to help work out his problem. That possibility had never occurred to me, but it made sense.

Without hesitation they ushered me into the temple's enormous library where huge bookshelves, ranging 20 to 30 feet high and separated by eight to ten foot aisles, extended for as far as I could see. Even though the floors were like clouds, they supported everything and provided firm footing.

Enormous leather-bound books of various colors, trimmed and edged with gold, filled the shelves. To me, the sight was marvelous.

As we walked down the aisles, my guides selected specific books and carried them to a very large table. There they opened the books and supplied the answers I sought. Intrigued by the beautiful calligraphy on the pages, I had to force myself to concentrate on the information being given to me. When my guides finished, they closed the books and returned them to the shelves. Then we left the library with the information I needed to pass on to the young man.

My guides escorted me to the place where I had entered, and we said goodbye knowing that I would return. I retraced my steps back along the cloud-like path and stepped off into space. Like jumping off a diving board into a swimming pool, I drifted downward. Although it felt as if I were falling rapidly, it was serene—no sensation of rushing wind against my body.

In the twinkling of an eye, I was again standing on my roof, and seeing myself in the rocking chair below. Quickly I slipped into my physical body.

I was home!

But this was only the beginning of a new journey for us. For this was my first experience at the Akashic Records. I was going from the edge of all the light I had, and I was being taught how to fly. Many times since then I have been reminded of the words of Claire Norris: "When we walk to the edge of all the light we have, and take the step into the darkness of the unknown, we must believe one of two things will happen: there will be something solid for us to stand on, or we will be taught how to fly."

We had come into an experience that we knew very little about and there wasn't anything solid to stand on, so we had to learn how to fly. For many years we had studied the Bible, which had become a foundation for our faith, in addition to prayer, meditation and service to the people around us.

But going to the Akashic Records was so different. It was like a new beginning. We had to learn new lessens, new disciplines and new principals. Though this was fraught with uncertainties ("...darkness of the unknown..."), with nothing solid to stand on, we were learning how to fly.

Perhaps you will understand better what "learning how to fly" means to us in this context; a couple of our experiences may help. For instance, learning to fly would be like doing something we hadn't done before, like leaving my body and going to the Akashic Records. It just happened, without prior conscious knowledge or preparation. Another experience is when Doris directed me to project myself, in a reading on the subject, out to the archeological site in Arizona. I had never done anything like that, nor had Doris. Another might be when I projected myself down through solid earth at that site, to see if I could point out any artifacts to be found there. I didn't know if I could do anything like that. These things were like stepping "into the darkness of the unknown" and because I attempted something in which I feared I might fail, I was "taught how to fly."

So I had been out of my body, gone to the Akashic Records, met my guides, obtained helpful information for the young man, and returned home.

Chapter 2

A Time for Change

As soon as I opened my eyes, Doris announced that dinner was ready.

It seemed to me as if I must have been gone at least an hour, but a glance at my watch revealed that only five minutes had elapsed.

During our meal I calmly recounted my experience to Doris. As unusual as this experience was for us, Doris and I were not especially surprised by it. We both considered this another step in our spiritual growth.

We sent the information I received at the Records to the young man. Later, he responded that he had found the suggestions very helpful and timely.

Since that day in 1969, every time someone comes to me for help, I retrace my steps to the Akashic Records—and that's been more than 8,000 times now.

What a change this experience initiated in my life!

These events took place while I was still in the aerospace field, so I didn't have much time to develop this new ability. However, I saw it as an instrument of God to use to help people understand themselves and their lives on this Earth plane, while trying to help them become better acquainted with God. It wasn't an overnight development—it came a little at a time. As people came to me with their needs and longings, I stretched myself a little further to help them. To serve God more fervently and humanity more effectively has always been my desire.

As R.E. McMasters has said, "Change is often desirable, sometimes necessary, but always inevitable."

I agree with that. We are all looking for a change but do not always have the courage to take the necessary action to bring that change into our lives. In our case, it was a time for a change—in our outlook, our consciousness, our understanding of what we knew, and in the further application of the principles we had learned.

When change comes, we ought to be prepared for it. On March 17, 1970 while still in the aerospace industry, I had a dream. I dreamed I was a young boy walking up an inclined path with many other people. On the right side of the road, there was an old man in a gray flannel suit, wearing a gray felt hat who was sitting on a rock.

I walked over to him, and he said, "There is a change coming in your life."

Then I woke up.

A few months later, I had left the aerospace industry, and we moved to Santa Maria, California, to devote all of my time to the life readings. This was a dramatic change—from aerospace engineer to counselor. Within a year, this initial service developed into what we have called "life readings." Since then, with the help of Doris, I have given thousands of readings for people from all over the world.

Occasionally, Doris and I have had questions about our work and have used the readings to find answers. For example, we wondered what the word "Akashic" meant, and how the information was stored in the Records.

In our search through conventional literature, we didn't find very much, except that "Akashic" was Sanskrit, meaning "primary substance." It could also be used to describe principles of life, such as the cycles of birth and death. There also seemed to be a connection with karma and what results were manifested.

Karma, though, is nothing more than the law of cause and effect; whatever you sow, you will also reap. If you sow distrust, resentment, and ill feelings, the same will return to you. The identical law will, of course, be in effect when you maintain a positive attitude. In bringing goodwill to those around you, you will receive the equivalent in return.

I decided to do a reading, hoping to gain a clearer picture of the role of the Akashic Records in our lives, and we received the following information.

The Akashic are records which each soul, who has passed from the physical into the non-physical, has deposited in a collective place, so they will have the opportunity to go over their own lives or their immediate past life. In so doing they may learn from it and recognize where the pitfalls have been. At the same time they will be able to understand that they have had some successes and not allow them to go to their heads.

We learned that the Akashic Records consist of information about every soul who has ever lived on Earth. It is here where the individual soul can retreat in order to learn. Some people see these Records as contained in temples like the library while others see them in a different form. But whatever their appearance, the individual usually sees these Records from their present point of view—that is, the culture, the nation, the language, and the civilization in which the person lives.

The Akashic Records have been in existence for millions of years and will probably continue for many more. It is here where the individual will look after death, to see from his own records what should have been done, but was never attempted and what should not have been done but was done many, many times. In other words, the time to review, the time to re-evaluate, the time to learn from one's own mistakes and accomplishments has arrived for that soul.

There are also teachers with each soul or group of souls who will show them, in classrooms with many other souls what they have done and how they can learn to grow. But in all this learning process, there is also the companionship with other souls who have made the same mistakes. So it is not a matter of crying on each other's shoulder, but it is a matter of learning from one another and thus helping each other, so all can be better prepared at their next incarnation. The result is to recognize the karmic situations and consider how they may be resolved. Evidently, this is an important step in the growth of a soul.

It seems that each soul may also review its own Records from ancient past times to obtain a broader view of the actions or activities that are of concern. The soul may have the opportunity to learn about its limitations, weaknesses, strengths, or whatever else is needed to build a person with substance and integrated character.

Before a soul enters into another incarnation, that soul will again review its own records for as long as necessary in order to keep fresh in its mind what it needs to resolve. There is also a reminder from the teacher with whom the soul has been working, to point out what the soul needs to work on now and what not to become involved with.

When the soul then enters the Earth for another life experience, there is always the quiet voice from within to remind the person what is right and what is wrong, as well as to tell him/her whether or not he/she is in the right profession. If the individual listens to that quiet voice, the message is there, and all that is needed to do is to act upon it.

Chapter 3

Cries for Help

"Can you help me?"

The letter, like so many others, was a desperate plea for help. This time it was a distressed young mother in Oregon.

"My adopted youngest son can't sleep," read the letter. "He stays awake until after midnight every night and is up at 4 A.M. every day."

Not only did her son stay awake most of the night, he had been arrested for shop lifting and check forgery, and he was only seven years old. If that weren't enough, he would often set fire to his bedroom. During the evening when it became very quiet in his bedroom, his mother would check on him to see what he was up to. She never knew what she might find. This condition had gone on for several years, and she had nearly come to the end of her rope.

I finished the letter and my heart went out to this mother and her problem. I had no idea whether I would be able to help her son; it appeared to be an impossible case to me—but I tried. The information from the Akashic Records proved very interesting.

Among the recommendations that were given in the reading was for the mother to get some lavender sheets for his bed and pink pajamas for him to sleep in. She had no difficulty finding the lavender sheets, but pink pajamas—for a boy? Unable to find anything like that, she made them herself. As soon as she had them finished, she put the lavender sheets on his bed, and he put on the pink pajamas.

That night he slept straight through and didn't wake up until morning. All through the night it was quiet in his room, and his mother, remembering what had taken place before, expected more of the same. She checked on him every two hours, but all she found was her youngster peacefully asleep.

From that day on, his sleeping problem was solved. He loved his pink pajamas and wore them until he had grown so tall that the pajama pants hit him just below the knee. His mother helped him overcome his other problems, and he grew to become a fine young man.

Some time later she attended a seminar on the East Coast. The speaker was an obstetrician who mentioned an interesting point. When a light shines on the abdomen of a pregnant woman, the interior of her womb is a light mauve color—like a pink-lavender. After his lecture she spoke with him privately about the problem with her son and how the lavender sheets and pink pajamas calmed him and helped him sleep through the night. Intrigued, the doctor suggested that the boy had needed an environment of love and security that he had felt in his mother's womb. As it was, after his birth his biological mother found she couldn't take care of him, so abandoned him.

Another interesting report from a 61-year-old woman gives a glimpse of what a reading can bring out. Her comments follow: "Before this reading I had my natal chart done, and everything that Mr. Abrahamsen said (in the reading) agreed with the chart—my remoteness in relationships, fear, and strong will.

"I have also been rebirthed recently and realized that I did not want to be born. Only spirits guiding me to the birth enabled me to do it. The reading pointed this out strongly.

"Mr. Abrahamsen suggested that I was intuitive," she continued. "This I didn't have any conception of, but I can begin to see this possibility in that I have now different feelings in this area.

"He also pointed out in the reading my great distrust of and distance from God. I had not realized this but have been greatly helped by this revelation.

"The reading has been very powerful for me and I believe very accurate. In all my searchings it has been the most helpful, and it has helped me to see the accuracies in my chart and in my rebirthing sessions.

"Also the suggestions to read Brother Lawrence's book, which was in my library; the particular passage in (the epistle of) Romans 12:1-2, which I had on my kitchen window, and asking forgiveness of my husband from the 1600's have been very positive."

When we hear this kind of report from people it makes it all worthwhile.

At times, however, the information given in a reading does not seem to have any particular relevance to the one for whom it is intended. But as time goes by the importance of the information goes right to the core of the matter. Sometimes the information is ahead of its time. One may be puzzled by the reading at first because the meaning of the information is not understood, and the tendency may be to discard the entire reading as a bad experience. Then one day something happens, and listening to the reading may give a clue that helps shed some light on a particular situation.

That was the case in 1976. I had done a reading for a young man in his late teens at the request of his mother. Afterwards she asked her son if he wanted to listen to it, but he was always so busy and didn't think it was important.

Then, three months later his best friend committed suicide. Again, his mother suggested that now he may want to listen to his reading. He agreed because he felt so devastated by the death of his friend. The first part of his reading dealt with suicides and what takes place when they reach the other side. These souls meet special guides who are appointed to minister to them. Upon arrival they discover to their dismay that the problems they sought to escape are still with them. The intense mental and emotional pain is carried over, and the confusion only adds to it. Their guides help them to understand that they will be required to repeat the course until they can endure it, learn to overcome the problems, or rise above them. Situations and experiences in life are like courses one takes in college. There are lessons to learn from them and obstacles to overcome.

This information given in the reading opened this teenager's eyes to the knowledge that there was more to life than he could ever imagine. He listened and to this day his reading continues to have an impact on him.

"Aron Abrahamsen? Oh yeah, I had a reading from him some years ago. The tape is at home in a box of little remembered psychic, harp, astrological, and numerological readings from my more phenomenally-oriented spiritual stage."

This teacher had just returned from an Association for Research and Enlightenment (ARE) conference where one of the speakers, Harmon Bro, Ph.D., had mentioned our work. She wrote a letter to Dr. Bro telling him how the conference had helped her and how the reference to our readings had sparked a search for the earlier reading.

The letter continued, "When I got home, I went searching for the tape of the reading. I put it in my Walkman, put on the headset, and settled into my bed to listen again, after eight years, to a tape I had deemed too boring and convoluted to deal with. I had never even listened to the entire tape. I had just chalked up the cost of the reading as a dead loss.

"A few minutes into the tape, I sat bolt up in bed. Wow! There was the answer to my decade of unrest."

She explained that in 1979 when the tape was made, she was living and working in a western city where her husband had been transferred. Although she had taught for ten years, she couldn't find a teaching position. She took whatever work she could find in order to go back to school. She wanted to work with the terminally ill—especially children.

"I was feeling very out of pocket," her letter continues. "I had heard about Abrahamsen in my A.R.E. study group several years earlier. I got his address from a friend at Virginia Beach. I wrote and asked for a reading. I waited a long time, but finally it came. I was very disappointed when I listened to the first part of it because it made not one wit of sense to me. I was not even thinking in the direction it was suggesting. I didn't know what in the world had happened. Had he got me mixed up with someone else?

"He was talking about my mission in life being involved with the soil, and he told me to look into something called hydroponics (the science of growing plants in liquid solution containing the necessary minerals, instead of soil). I just ignored it, went my way, and got my MS degree."

Her letter details years of trying to follow her field but being side-tracked out of necessity. These so-called detours took her through countless experiences in high school science, gardening pursuits, and alternative habitats, until finally her interests piqued in earth science and hydroponics. Doors were opening to her on all sides in these fields. After having gone through so many frustrating detours from her original interests, the success in this new field almost frightened her. *Had she gotten too far off course,* she wondered, *or had she finally found her purpose?*

"Now, in the throes of self-doubt, terrified of success, I began again to search for purpose," she wrote to Dr. Bro, "My ego was so involved and so screwed up [when] I drove to the retreat that I was on the edge of suicide. I don't know why. Looking back, it makes no sense. But I came to your sessions seeking a word or a phrase that would put me in touch with my purpose. When it came, I didn't recognize it. When I applied it later, I was shocked at how blind I had been to it all those years.

"Eight years ago, a psychic in Washington State had spoken of the soil and teaching others to survive on their own plots of land, using hydroponics and food preservation. What I didn't even consider then is part and parcel of my life today. And every door has been opened along the way. Everything I have asked for has come to the project.

"Listening to that tape affirmed that I am actually moving toward what I am supposed to do in this life. You must know that great anguish and anxiety dropped away from me with that realization. A calm has come over me that I have not known for a very long time. I have no idea where it will lead."

She concludes by writing, "Thank you, Dr. Bro, for being there at the retreat to share yourself with us. Thank you for saying the right name—Abrahamsen! Thanks to Aron Abrahamsen for speaking across the years to me and helping me free my mind to work on my work."

It's reports like this from those who we have given readings that offer us our special rewards. It reinforces the decision we made those many years ago to help people through the readings. Although the recipient may be unaware of it at the time of the reading, the message contained in his or her reading is very personal and individual.

We remain confident that the information from the Akashic Records is dealing specifically with the person's mission and often their cry for help.

From my own experience of great need, loneliness and inner cries for help when I first came to this country, my spirit had become sensitive to the cries of others in need. How very satisfying it has been to me to know that my service to God has been that of helping others. For since early in 1940, He has sent so many to help me.

Chapter 4

Healing of Memories

Since my first experiences at the Akashic Records, friends asked if I had ever had psychic experiences as a child. As I recall, my childhood was no more unusual than other young boys growing up in Norway in the pre-war Europe of the 1930's.

To my recollection I can't remember any experiences which I would classify as psychic, except one event which probably signaled the recall of a past life.

Reflecting on it today, it is interesting to discover how a problem from a past life can be a block for further growth in the present lifetime. But, as I found out, when the source, not the symptom, of a problem is revealed, it is easier to resolve that conflict. In this case all that was necessary was to forgive those who were involved—then move on. This healing experience seemed to open my understanding to the importance of resolving inner conflicts. I believe that the unresolved problems tend to move in and out of our consciousness as a thread being woven into a fabric and developing a pattern that causes disharmony in our life.

In my case it was a great encouragement to find that the source of a conflict could be dealt with whether it was in this present life or in a previous one. That one experience may have seemed confusing at the time, but later it made perfect sense. I had gone to a movie theater to see "A Midsummer Night's Dream." I was 16 years old and had no idea what the movie was about. From the beginning to the end of the movie I sat spellbound. The music sounded so familiar, yet I didn't recall having ever heard it.

On the way home, I whistled every passage of the entire score, and I pictured in my mind every instrument as it played some particular selection. On an inner level, I knew that I must have been very familiar with that composition at some time, but I didn't trouble myself then about where or when it might have been.

I always kept in my mind that event, and it was brought back to my memory every time I heard that overture. The solution came in a roundabout way.

I had a prejudice toward the Japanese that I could neither reconcile nor explain. So a few years after I had opened my mind to reincarnation, I decided to find out why I had such a dislike for the Japanese. Vividly, I remembered how much I despised them when I was in Japan during the Korean War. I didn't like their language, their music and, least of all, their customs. I was furious at them for being so strange and unfriendly. On the other hand, I made no attempt to befriend them because I rejected the idea of having these seemingly strange people as my friends.

I supposed that my hostility could be a result of their attack on Pearl Harbor. I couldn't remember that any one of them had ever done anything to me personally—so why all this animosity?

It was the summer of 1969 that I projected myself, in meditation, back to my immediate past life and found myself in England in the 1860's. I was a prosperous merchant and had made arrangements with a sailing vessel for passage to Australia for a business trip. En route the ship ran into a violent storm in the Pacific Ocean and blew the vessel far to the north. The wind and waves battered the ship relentlessly, and eventually it capsized. Japanese fishermen found me clinging to debris and calling for help. They picked me up and brought me to shore, where I was arrested and thrown into a crowded prison. Several months went by in that rat-infested, dark and unsanitary hole. I survived on a small bowl of unsavory food and water that was passed to me once a day.

Eventually I was released and sailed back to England. I never got to Australia. The recall of this past life experience brought to light the source of my aversion for the Japanese—I had been mistreated, and my subconscious mind wouldn't let me forget. If I could forgive my Japanese captors, I would be free from that karma.

The words of Jesus kept running through my mind: "And ye shall know the truth, and the truth shall make you free." (John 8:32)

The truth of the matter was finally revealed. I immediately forgave those who held me in prison. Instantly, I felt a great relief and peace over this traumatic situation. It was as if a light had been turned on within me. I no longer felt angry towards the Japanese; rather, I felt a strong urge to know these people better. I longed to cultivate an interest in their music, language and culture.

That opportunity came in 1977 when Doris and I traveled to Japan; I was very much at home in that environment and learned to love the people.

In that same meditation, almost as a bonus, I discovered the source of my fascination with Mendelssohn's overture. I learned that I had been an amateur musician, too, and played the violin in a small orchestra in England. This was a very pleasant period of my life. While playing in that orchestra, I first heard the overture. During my Japanese imprisonment, strains of that overture played over and over in my mind, helping me maintain my sanity and survive that difficult experience.

We have learned from the Akashic Records that when we hold resentment and other negative emotions in our minds and hearts, we keep alive that which will eventually destroy us. This impressed upon us the importance of finding the source of any negative emotions and dealing with them by asking and extending forgiveness.

Having the experience from Japan healed in this way is what many have come to refer to as the *healing of memories*. This is done by projecting ourselves in meditation back to the incident we are troubled about. Then we visualize the episode as we understand it to be. Healing begins as forgiveness is extended. As this forgiving experience takes place, it is then imprinted on our subconscious mind as having actually occurred. That's what happened here. Finally, the mysteries surrounding the Mendelssohn composition and my loathing of the Japanese were unraveled and resolved.

But the real value to the gift that we had discovered was not so much what it meant to us. More importantly, it opened up a path for us to be more helpful to others. In the beginning we did not know the limits of this phenomenon, so it was a matter of experimentation.

One of our early readings also dealt with healing of the memories. It was one that I did for a young housewife.

She had been married for several years and had two small children and a wonderful husband. They lived in a well-to-do neighborhood, and seemingly everything was going their way. But not quite.

It all started one day when a friend of ours, a Presbyterian minister, called and said he had been counseling this woman for several months but had been unable to make any further progress.

She had attempted suicide several times, he said, because she just didn't like her husband, and this was her way of resolving her dilemma. My friend asked if I could do a reading for her to see if any information could be made available to help her. When he had finished, I immediately protested because I had never done anything like that before, and I didn't know if I could be of any help. I tried to refuse, but he insisted. Finally, I agreed to at least try.

The information I received showed that at one time she had been in India in a very influential and wealthy family. At a very early age she had been married to a man much older than she, and this marriage had been pre-arranged by the parents from the time she was born, which was a common occurrence. The marriage was an absolute disaster to her. She hated her husband, found no purpose in living, and tried to kill herself several times. But each time was unsuccessful. Her husband in India was the same one she was married to in this present life.

I sent this information on a cassette tape to my friend who would use it in counseling this woman.

As soon as the tape arrived, arrangements were made for another session with the young housewife. She listened to the tape and immediately identified herself with the young bride in India, married to the same husband she had in this life. As she listened, she started to cry and realized that the memory from the past had been carried over to the present time. She had the same feelings and needs then as now. The hopelessness and emptiness were still with her as it had been in India so many years ago.

She now knew the source of her despair. With help from our friend, she could forgive her parents and herself for the past. Our friend counseled her about the attitude she held towards her marriage in India and how that might prevent her from having a successful marriage in the present.

Her memory from the past was healed. After that, she no longer had difficulty with that part of her life. Her relationship with her husband improved and she was like a new person.

It was gratifying to us that we had been able to help someone whom we had never seen nor known, and to this day we have never met her. As it has turned out, the majority of the thousands of readings we have done, have been for those we have never seen or known.

Chapter 5

Learning Episodes

As the years went on, I gained more confidence in knowing that what I was doing was right for me, at that time. It was like wearing the right size suit in the right color. It was a perfect fit. Every time I did a reading, it was a new experience, no matter how many I had completed. I had learned and am still learning, never to take anything for granted. I love helping people in whatever way I can.

My first experience at the Akashic Records was only the beginning of a new period of growth. I have retraced my steps there many, many times and have learned so much—and expect to continue learning.

We can learn from many sources as long as we are willing. The opportunities are everywhere. To learn and grow is an exciting experience filled with enthusiasm and uncertainties—enthusiasm about the new things we discover but uncertainty because of the changes that come with growth.

We also learned that nobody on this planet knows everything about all things. We accept that and consider it normal. Who could be so wise as to have all knowledge? However, I believe we do have access to all knowledge if we can tap into it as a human being on this planet.

But how is it on the so-called *other side?* Do those on that side know everything? At one time I thought they did but have since discovered that it isn't so.

That point was brought to my attention quite vividly at some of my visits to the Akashic Records.

One was when I was doing a research reading on a scientific theme. On this occasion I had gone to the Akashic Records and told my guides I was looking for some very specific technical information. While I was talking to them, several people began appearing on the porch of the temple where we were until a group of 30 were assembled. I asked one of them for an answer to my question.

An answer was given, and then the other 29 also gave me answers. But they were all different. The whole scene became very confusing and disturbing.

In the midst of all this commotion, Christ appeared on the porch. He recognized the situation for what it was and took immediate charge.

He turned to the group, looked at everyone and asked them if any of them knew what they were talking about. Like one voice all of them said no. Then Christ asked why they attempted to answer my question if they didn't know the subject matter.

It seems that they had been in the neighborhood and had heard that I was searching for an answer to my question. They were more than happy to accommodate me.

"We have lots of answers," one of them said, "and perhaps one of them may fit his question. We had nothing else to do, and would like to have helped."

Upon hearing all this, Christ dismissed the group.

What I had failed to do when the large group appeared, was to challenge them and ask if they were experts on the subject in order for me to determine if they could give me the correct information. But I must have been flattered when so many people gathered around me. I thought, for sure, I must be important but I'd forgotten the most vital step.

In this session I discovered there were souls on the non-physical plane who were experts in particular areas. If I needed some expert advice in the field of astronomy, I would ask for those with competence in these areas. This is the same as there are specialists, or experts, in specific disciplines on this physical plane.

An expert on the subject was then called in.

When he arrived I challenged him before posing the question for which I had come. He passed the challenge.

The concept of challenging comes from the Edgar Cayce readings, where he would challenge entities he encountered on the other side. I read that information with great interest and decided to use it when I would encounter entities during the process of giving a reading.

The challenge was to insure that I was protected from any unwanted entities and to make sure I met with trustworthy souls who would supply me with correct information.

The challenge itself is very simple. When I am on the other side and approached by someone, I use the challenge as follows:

First, I ask the entity if he comes in the name of Christ. If the entity answers, "Yes," I ask the second question: "Do you believe that Jesus Christ has come in the flesh?"

If the answer is *yes* to the second question, I am confident that I will receive the correct information. Then I can begin to listen to what is being said. But I also must be aware that no entity knows everything, and there are limits to what knowledge it has.

Should the answer be *no* to any of these questions, I suggest that he/she go to the Messenger of Light.

Over the years I have found this method of challenging very useful and practical. I know of no other method that is as effective as the one I've mentioned. I also am aware that when I challenge whomever I meet on the other side and I receive affirmative answers to both questions, I know I will receive reliable information.

This was the case with an expert who was called in. A man in English clothing appeared. At my request he then gave his name from his immediate past incarnation which, as well as I can remember, was John Wilkins and said that he had lived in England in the 1600's. He indicated that in his day, he was interested in the possible planetary influences on earthquakes.

Having confidence I would receive answers of integrity, I asked him about the relationship between earthquakes and the position of the planets with respect to Earth. He told me he had written several treatises on that very subject during his life in England, and that he would return in the future to prove the correctness of his theory.

Later, the person for whom the reading was done found the expert's name in Who's Who in Science, which stated that he had lived in England at the time he claimed. During that lifetime he had received a doctorate from Cambridge and had written several books, some of which were on the subject of astronomy.

The information which I obtained from this gentleman proved to be very accurate and interesting to my client.

On another of my early trips to the Akashic Records my two guides told me that they would teach me as much as they knew, after which I'd be assigned another pair of guides.

That experience with the thirty entities took the wind out of my sails. I had assumed for so many years that everybody on the other side knew everything and needed no more teaching, but I was wrong.

I discovered that just because a person makes the transition to the non-physical world, it doesn't mean he suddenly "knows all." Actually, he/she is as ignorant or wise, as he/she was before. Leaving planet Earth does not give instant learning, wisdom, or knowledge. Going through the transition is not an entrance to wisdom. The old saying "As a tree falls, so it lies" applies very well here.

I was told that those who make the transition are as interested in what they were doing and in the people they associated with—such as family and friends—as when they were in the physical body. The only thing that has changed is the environment. They think, they feel, and they are concerned over those who are left behind. If there are people they have resented while in the physical body, these resentments are still with them on the other side. Such episodes didn't discourage me from returning to the Akashic Records; however, for it was an important learning experience for me, and others reported that it was a great help and comfort to them.

A number of readings later, when I returned to the Records, a change took place that shouldn't have surprised me. But it did.

Chapter 6

Changing of the Guides

About three years after my initial experience at the Akashic when I came to the familiar fork in the road, normally I would turn left, but this time I kept going straight. I just felt that it was time to explore this path. It brought me to a different approach to the temple.

When I had entered from the porch previously, I always assumed it was the front door. However, looking at the temple from this viewpoint, I realized that I had not been seeing the main entrance at all. I'd seen the side door!

Directly in front of me was a long, narrow stairway made from pure white marble and lined on both sides with rose bushes. As usual, it was very quiet. I climbed the stairway. At the top I met two guides—not my usual ones. They introduced themselves as my new guides. These were my third set.

I greeted them. One was a Chinese gentleman and the other a Greek. The Chinese man wore a black skull cap, his hair was drawn back into a pigtail which extended down his back. A very decorative kimono made from black silk and hand-embroidered in a very beautiful design covered the very slender and short figure.

The other guide wore a short white toga. Both were apparently good friends because they appeared to get along quite well. Now they were going to give me some assistance.

The Chinese guide took charge and presented the new routine I was to follow. Whenever I came to the records, I would present myself to them before entering the main library.

"We will give you some advice, when needed each time you come here," he said, "but for the most part you are now on your own." I was told very precisely that I would be observed and possibly offered suggestions.

They would not go with me into the library to search for information. They would remain on the outside, available if I needed help.

I was also cautioned that just because I was now being allowed to enter through the main entrance, I should not become *high-minded* about it.

The first time I arrived at the records, I remembered that my two guides were waiting for me. They escorted me into the library and did all the work for me.

After that, each time I came to the records, my guides told me what to look for in the books as they watched closely over my shoulder. I was corrected on a number of occasions, and I learned to be more careful and accurate. Then one day my guides said they were leaving. They had been transferred to some other place where they could teach someone else.

Knowing this, I wasn't surprised when one day I arrived at the records by the side entrance to find another set of guides. I asked them what had happened to my first set of guides, and the new guides said they had been transferred to another place. That was the last I ever saw of them, and I wonder what they are doing now.

My second set of guides taught me how to interpret symbols and colors. It was a very interesting course of instruction which lasted several months. Every day I would meet with them, and they would show me how I should handle the meaning of symbols and what colors meant in connection with the symbols. Day after day I retraced my steps to the records, met my two guides, and the teaching session would begin as I obtained information for a reading.

A year later when I arrived at the records, I noticed my guides were troubled. I asked them why, and they told me that they too were being reassigned to another part of the Akashic.

That was the day before I entered via the straight path and along a staircase flanked with roses.

I asked my Chinese guide, "Why the rose bushes?"

His answer was simple and not very profound, "I like roses."

I thought that was interesting because roses are my favorite flowers, too.

Now I was on my own, so to speak. I felt a bit apprehensive but took courage in the good tutoring I had received. I was determined to apply all I had learned.

Chapter 7

Reaching into the Unknown

It was a simple request. The letter was from a young man who wanted information on where he could excavate human skeletons on this continent earlier than 100,000 years, He lived on the East Coast and apparently had an interest in archaeology. Other than his name and address, I knew nothing about him.

His initial letter said he had visited the headquarters of the Association for Research and Enlightenment (ARE), the Edgar Cayce organization and had met some people who suggested he contact me for a life reading.

The information from the reading pointed out that in earlier life times he had been interested in geology and had written several papers on ancient civilizations, as well as being a teacher in ancient history.

In Egypt, in the 300 B.C., he was an interpreter for the foreign people who would come to the Court in that country. He was also an interpreter for both the common people and higher ups. They spoke different dialects. He was able to interpret the people's languages, as well as draw benefit from the trade. He was interested in geological functions, in the stone structure, as well as the various strata in the Egyptian soil, as well as those in the land of Palestine, and in the surrounding country.

Then in another past life in Palestine, during the time of Christ, the readings say that this man was a carpenter, a furniture builder.

His talent in Palestine was mainly in objects of antiquity, the items that would be called excavations of old/archaeology, as well as the modern furnishings. His spiritual ascent in that life was such that though he was eager to investigate many archaeological areas; spiritually, he needed to learn the value of commitment so he could be settled and anchored in having the correct foundation.

Another time he was in England in the 1600's. Here he was a writer of documents, hand-written, of course. These documents were of ancient civilizations. He was a teacher of ancient history and also a teacher of those things that call for the necessities in the clothing, culture, political, as well as the economic life. He taught at a school in London, and his interest was more in ancient times in past civilizations than in the present, so he lives, so to speak, in the past neglecting the present.

The next life and the last that was given, was in the 1820's to 1860. He was a mighty warrior in an Indian tribe in Arizona.

In his reply to us, he expressed his astonishment and was amazed at the accuracy of his first reading. He further stated that he had a professional degree in geological engineering from Colorado School of Mines, a Masters degree in business administration (M.B.A.) from Columbia University and would be pursuing a doctorate in anthropology.

In follow-up readings, which were among 30 eventually taken, he requested where he might excavate to find evidence of very early civilizations. Three areas were given: Mexico, Colorado, and northern and central Arizona. A few weeks later, I received a second request from him, asking for details on the area in Arizona.

The information from that reading was given in detail, describing the geology and rock formation in that area, the climatic conditions in ancient past times, and types of people who had lived there.

He also stated that the reason for choosing the Arizona site was because he had been accepted at the University of Arizona in Tucson to work toward a Ph.D. in Anthropology. The Flagstaff site area was close enough to enable him to excavate for early artifacts of homo sapiens while he continued his schooling.

This made me a little nervous. What if he didn't find anything? After all, I had never done anything like this before. Was this kind of information within the range of the capabilities of this gift? I wanted, of course, to help him in his efforts to uncover positive proof of early civilization, but the words "what if" kept racing through my mind.

In September 1971, another reading was given where graphic information was obtained as to where to dig in order to find some potsherds of an earlier civilization.

He called me one morning reporting that he and a group of people had traveled from Tucson to Flagstaff and had started to dig in the area I had indicated—but they found nothing. He was calling from a payphone and needed to know right away where to dig. Snow was falling so time was of essence.

I told him to call me back in three hours so I could do a *check reading* for him to determine if the area where he was digging really was the right place. A check reading is just another reading, usually very short in length, on the same subject to make sure that the information from the previous reading was accurate.

After I had finished the three scheduled readings for that morning, and while I was still in a deep meditation, Doris initiated something new for me. She directed me to go to the site where they were digging and describe the area. I projected myself to the location of the dig and described everything I saw in a circle of 360 degrees. I saw everything very clearly and in every detail. Then I discovered their problem in not finding the potsherds that were indicated in the reading. They were five feet too far to the south of where these potsherds would be located. I gave the new direction and said confidently that now they would find what they had come for. All of this was tape recorded.

Three hours later he called back, and I played the tape recording over the phone. When it was finished, I asked him if the area I described was anything like it really was.

All he said was, "You were there."

He then asked me if I had seen a stake in the ground right by where I had been standing. I told him I didn't, which puzzled him. I didn't understand the importance of this question. Since there was nothing more to discuss, he hung up and hurried out to the site.

A few hours later he called again, and the laughter in his voice told me he had found what had been predicted. He also said that the stake he had pounded into the ground before making the first call was not there when he returned after obtaining the corrected direction. While he was making the phone call, somebody, not thinking it was important, had removed the stake and put it into the truck. The mystery of the missing stake was solved.

The young archaeologist and his group happily left Flagstaff to return to Tucson. However, he returned the next summer and started some serious excavations in hopes of finding some artifacts that would indicate the presence of an early civilization.

In the early days of the many readings I did for him, he experimented with me. Perhaps at that time, he felt this was necessary to satisfy himself that I would be able to supply the information he was looking for.

During that time we were living in southern Oregon, and he asked me to find his house in Tucson, Arizona, and give him a description of it. I did and described his house and the area where he lived. At the same time I gave him a local weather report. I also looked into his storage shed and told him it needed to be cleaned out.

In the spring of 1972, he invited Doris and me to Tucson and took us out to the site, which was in the San Francisco Mountains just outside Flagstaff. Here a reading was taken. Foot by foot, information was given as to what would be discovered, if that area were ever excavated.

Over the next three years, he found 55 out of 58 anticipated artifacts in the exact position stated in the reading and at the predicted levels. Later, he wrote a book entitled, *Psychic*

Archeology, (now out of print) about his experiences, and included the results of that series of readings.

During the time when we were at the proposed excavation site in Flagstaff, he buried an item about twenty-five feet away from where I was sitting and asked me to describe it. It was the rear left bone from a dog, which I described correctly. This last experiment took place just before the reading that predicted what he would find at certain levels during his proposed excavation.

Over the years I have grown weary of researchers trying to prove to themselves that valid information can be obtained by remote viewing, so I no longer participated in these types of experiments. After all, the life readings took all of my time.

But in the beginning, especially with the archeologist, it was interesting to discover how far my abilities could reach.

Chapter 8

Guidance for Daily Living

It's not supernatural. The quest for guidance is more a learning of how to listen, being alert to signs, trusting those signs, and finally acting upon one's intuitive judgement. Even before I understood astral projection or started giving readings, we pursued guidance and received it.

Over the years Doris and I have sought God's guidance and tried to act on that guidance once it had been given. During our trek along this spiritual passage, we've discovered many tools and disciplines useful for our growth and development. Meditation has been helpful. So has prayer. We have grown through Bible study, church membership, and being available when others have needed help and comfort. We have worked to apply the principles we have absorbed.

All along the path we opened ourselves to the possibility that God would guide us as he did those in ancient times, and it was exhilarating just considering the possibilities.

As we remember it, we first became aware of special guidance when we lived in Long Beach, CA. Aron had been working for an engineering firm near downtown Los Angeles. That meant at least an hour's drive, to work each morning through bumper to bumper traffic. And, of course, the same again coming home after work.

Aron's nerves were becoming frayed from all this stress, so we determined that he should seek another engineering firm in circumstances easier for us to handle. After sitting down together with paper and pen, we thought about what would be the optimum situation for him. We came up with three stipulations for his next job: 1) to live in a small town; 2) be near a large town—for the social and cultural opportunities it would offer; and 3) have only a ten minute drive to work from home.

We prayed and asked God to help us find such a place. Also, as I was listening to the radio one morning soon after, a religious program was offering to pray with people for their needs if they would call the phone number that was given. I called that number and told them what we were praying for. The person on the end of the line prayed in detail, as we had, right there while I was on the line. I was touched; tears came to my eyes.

The packing for our move had already begun. As Aron looked for companies up the coast, they all appeared to be located in the large cities. Finally, Aron decided to apply for work at Ryan Aeronautical in San Diego since it was by the bay. We drove there the next day. I sat in the car in their parking lot while Aron was being interviewed. He was with them for quite a while, and the end of the work day was upon us. I watched the four-lane highway outside the parking lot become heavy with traffic. My heart sank as I began to fear that this could be just as bad as before.

Soon Aron came to the car and said that he was offered an engineering job with Ryan. He was excited about it. When I asked about all the traffic, he said that he had inquired about where he might find an apartment in a small town that would be nearby. He learned that there were apartments in a little town near by called Ocean Beach. He got directions, and we headed over that way immediately.

The directions took us up a steep hill on a street called Narraganset. When we reached the top and started down ,we were faced with a gorgeous view of the ocean. It took our breath away! At the bottom of Narraganset was Sunset Cliffs Boulevard, and toward the right was a little street that led right out to the beach. That fulfilled part of our prayer. Going left on Sunset Cliffs Boulevard. we came to an area that was practically on the cliffs. On that little street there was a triplex where an apartment was for rent. Liking what we saw, we asked the owner how far it was to

Ryan. (We hadn't paid attention coming over the hill.) She didn't know, so we asked her would she hold the apartment for us until we drove over there to see how long it would take. She was very accommodating. We set out to retrace our steps back to the gates at Ryan. It took us exactly ten minutes!

Upon returning to the apartment, we asked the lady how far was it to San Diego. She said it was about twenty minutes. Everything was just what we had prayed for! We took the apartment and drove back to Long Beach to finish packing and place our house for sale. Two weeks later, we moved to San Diego.

Our experience with guidance has been very important to us because it has revealed what decisions to make and when to make them—and when to wait. It taught us to listen from within and hear the messages spoken to us. Especially we found in the Bible, a rich source of principles to apply to our lives which proved priceless for guidance. We also learned to test the principles, making sure we were on the right track before we stepped out—like putting out a fleece. That principle comes from the book of Judges, (Judges 6:36-40), where God called Gideon to be the leader of His people. At first, Gideon resisted the responsibility because he felt inadequate. However, he knew that if God wanted him to be the leader, he couldn't fail. But Gideon had to be sure, so he devised a test for verification. He asked God to show him in a very unique way. Gideon put out a lamb's fleece that night. In the morning, if the ground around the fleece was dry and the fleece wet, Gideon would believe that God, in fact, had chosen him to lead His people.

The next morning the fleece was wet with dew, but the ground was dry. That was a remarkable answer, but Gideon needed to be positive. Gideon spoke to God again. This time when Gideon put out the fleece, he requested that it would be dry and the ground wet.

The following morning, Gideon found the fleece dry, but the ground around it was wet. This gave Gideon the assurance that he should be the leader of the people.

Doris and I have followed this principle whenever we had difficulty discerning the will of God. No, we don't use a lamb's fleece like Gideon, but there are other ways of putting out a fleece.

In 1958 I was working for a company that had relocated my division to Denver, Colorado. Key employees were transferred with all moving expenses paid. Everyone told us Denver was a choice area, and that we would love it. With high expectations we agreed to go and rented a house in the area until we could decide in what part of the city we would settle.

It was summer and the weather was hot. We were very uncomfortable—we can't tolerate too much heat. As it turned out, we didn't find Denver to be as attractive as we were told.

In California we had lived very close to the ocean, and here we felt like fish out of water. It was in Denver that we realized how important the ocean was to us. We missed it terribly and wished we were back in California. A number of the others who also had been transferred with us were sorry that they had come to Denver, each for a different reason. We all inquired about transferring back to the Los Angeles area, but the company vetoed it. The only way to get back to the West Coast, it seemed, was to quit and find another job in California. Some did just that.

However, we had prayed about the move to Denver prior to arriving, and were certain that this was right for us. We assumed, therefore, there was something for us to learn before leaving Denver.

Coincidentally, we had discovered an organization called The Navigators in Colorado Springs that taught people how to study the Bible on their own, so Doris and I enrolled. We gained considerable help and encouragement as the teachers schooled us in how to set up daily spiritual disciplines. We learned that discipleship was not just daily Bible study, prayer, and meditation. It was equally important that we live a life of wholesome thought, speech, and behavior, and by faith apply God's principles to our lives. This was the beginning of serious spiritual disciplines for us. We were convinced that this experience must have been the reason we had been transferred to Denver.

Back at the office, the project that I was working on was bogged down. After three months of hectic and intense work, a design problem had put the project behind schedule. I had an idea for a complete redesign of the entire project that would solve the problem, so I made preparations to recommend these changes at the next regular meeting in Los Angeles.

Before leaving for the meeting in Los Angeles, Doris and I prayed. We talked to God as we would to a highly respected friend and asked that if we had learned in Denver what we came for, would He give us a sign that He was ready to move us back to the West Coast. We put out a fleece as a sign.

My suggestion for the fleece was that one of the engineers (whom I knew would meet me in the lobby of the building where the meeting was to take place) would say, "Aron, the best thing for this project would be for the company to bring it back to Los Angeles."

When I arrived at the lobby of the building in Los Angeles, one of the engineers I had worked with came over to me, and said "Aron, the best thing for this project would be for the company to bring it back to Los Angeles."

I knew in my heart that God had answered our prayer, and that we were about to move back to the West Coast.

During the meeting where my design proposal had been presented, the chief engineer announced that he wanted the project back in Los Angeles—and that he wanted me to come with it.

We only had seven days to get ready to be transferred back to Los Angeles. I called Doris that evening. I said, "Start packing!"

We had put out a fleece, and it worked.

We don't always seek for guidance that way, but when we believe the occasion warrants it, we employ that technique.

Although we were already believers that God answers prayers, this experience convinced us that God was eager to guide us in our daily decisions. It was a way of making us develop our intuition and recognize that everything in our being needs to be stretched so that we can begin to see a little further ahead on our path.

We have discovered that timing can be very crucial and that action is often required without hesitation. It is a matter of believing that what God says is true, and all that's needed is for us to follow up on what's been told us.

That was the case when I was working for General Dynamics in San Diego. I had been assigned to a department that wasn't using my talents. I looked into another one which needed my skills and was invited to transfer to it. They had the kind of work that I would enjoy. I would have to initiate the transfer through my department manager, and I was eager to make the change.

Wanting to discern the correct timing for this, I was praying for the right opportunity to approach the manager so that the transfer could be accomplished in the shortest possible time.

Several weeks had gone by, and nothing had happened. I had sought for some awareness from God about it, but all was quiet. Then one morning when I was attending a professional conference in Los Angeles, as was my custom, I got up extra early to read the Bible. I continued reading where I had left off the day before and began reading about God telling Elijah to go and see Ahab (I Kings 18:1).

I connected this scene with my situation immediately. I needed to know when to see the department manager to request the transfer. Ahab was the symbol of a man in high authority. My department manager was a man in high authority in my situation. God had shown me through this passage that now was the right time.

When I came back to my office in San Diego, I went right away to see the manager. He was on vacation. Had I misunderstood? Was the timing wrong? I found his assistant and stated my request. He immediately agreed to the transfer, and asked when I wanted to make the change. By the end of the day all the paperwork had been processed, and I was in the department I wanted.

Later I learned that if I *had* seen the department manager for a transfer, he would have opposed it because he was known never to allow anyone to transfer from his department. He didn't want to lose any of his men.

The timing was right!

We learned through many years of experience how to discern the will of God. From applying spiritual principles we learned that developing the inner being requires every part of our life to be involved. That meant to us that there needs to be a balance between the physical, intellectual, emotional, and spiritual aspects of ourselves. We could see that this would assure a balanced development with less likelihood of making irrational detours.

In our spiritual quest for God, we have come across many experiences that have helped us focus on the necessity of using every part of our being to reach our goal.

I remember another experience that took place while we were still living in San Diego. Doris and I felt led to provide a center for youth groups and a retreat place for some of our missionary friends, so they could get away to rest on their furloughs. Earlier, we had gone on vacation to a resort at Big Bear Lake in the San Bernardino Mountains 120 miles east of Los Angeles. While there, we wondered if this could be the area where God would have the center.

One morning as we studied the Bible, Doris read, "Go in and possess the land. The Lord your God hath given you rest and hath given you this land" (Joshua 1:11, 13). We felt that God was telling us that this was the place.

The same day we contacted a realtor who showed us several cabins. None were suitable. Our search continued the next day. The realtor showed us a large rustic lodge called Midori Land. Was this the *land* God had spoken to us about? We thought maybe this was it.

The property had 300 feet on the lake, and the lodge had 5000 square feet of living space under one roof. It seemed to fit all our criteria, but it was much larger—and more expensive—than we had contemplated. The price was *out of sight* as far as we were concerned, especially since we still had to live and work in San Diego.

We told the realtor we had to think about it.

Back in San Diego, we were a little disappointed that we hadn't seen anything suitable in our price range. It seemed as if God had encouraged us only to let us down with a hard thump.

A few months later as I was reading the Bible I came across this: "How long are you slack to go in to possess the land which the Lord God of your fathers has given you?"(Joshua 18:3). I felt embarrassed for doubting. I told God that I would even sell our home and move up there if that was needed. Doris was a bit shocked to hear me promise that, but she agreed that she would be amenable to do whatever God required of us.

The realtor in Big Bear Lake was glad to hear from us. She presented our offer to buy the lodge, contingent upon the sale of our house, and the offer was accepted. We immediately offered our house for sale. We knew that I would have to quit my job, if and when, we moved.

That was November, and the real estate market in our area was stagnant. Several homes had been for sale for a number of years. That wasn't very encouraging. However, we believed that if it was God's plan for us to buy Midori Land, He would bring us a buyer. And that's the way we prayed. If our house didn't sell, we would remain in San Diego, and that was okay with us because we loved it there. If, on the other hand, the house did sell, we would move to Midori Land. What we wanted was God's will for us.

Then early one Sunday morning as I was reading the Bible, I came across a passage which sprang out at me: "Prepare thee stuff for removing and remove by day in their sight; and thou shalt remove from thy place to another place in their sight" (Ezekiel 12:3).

Doris and I both believed that God had given us packing orders to move to Big Bear Lake, but the sale of our house that day would put His final approval on our move. We were away from home all day, and it rained a heavy downpour all day. Had we been wrong thinking the house would sell that day? Maybe so. We went to bed.

Early the next morning—at 7 A.M.—our realtor called. Our home had sold the day before. It had been on the market for less than thirty days.

Two months later we moved to Big Bear Lake.

During that whole period, we had used all of our faculties to determine if this move was right. We used our physical energies to contact realtors and look at properties. We used our intellect and emotional energies in not allowing our own desires to influence our spiritual disciplines, and maintain a proper perspective of the whole matter. We had continued our daily spiritual disciplines of praying in the early morning, reading the Bible, and meditating on the Word of God.

Our discernment and insight have been sharpened as we've learned to be alert to the many ways God has chosen to guide us in our daily life.

We used the readings for seeking guidance in our own lives as well. The move to Santa Maria (CA) was the result of guidance, which was obtained from a reading for us.

In it we were told to go first to Santa Maria for a year or so and then to Southern Oregon (southwest of Medford to an area with a river and trees) for three to five years. Then we would move to our final destination.

During the reading Doris asked why we couldn't go to the final destination first and avoid the other two moves. We were told there were lessons we needed to learn in each place. One lesson was to learn what was needed to establish ourselves in our new work, and this turned out to be correct.

In Santa Maria we were advised in the reading not to buy property but just rent for a year. From there we went to Applegate, Oregon, which is southwest of Medford. The property there extended to the middle of the Applegate River on one end and into forested land on the other end. We built our house on a hillside overlooking the lovely Applegate Valley.

A little more than three years later, we moved to the state of Washington, where we lived in sight of Puget Sound, as well as the Cascade Mountains.

God gives us many tools for unearthing His guidance. We find that if we follow that guidance, we will eventually accomplish our life's purpose. Always along the winding pathway, we learn the lessons of life required to accomplish that goal.

At another time, assurance through guidance was obtained but in a round about way. We had been living in Santa Maria a few months when I became very concerned whether what I was doing (giving readings) would ever supply our material needs. Would our economic needs be taken care of? Would I be able to earn enough from this type of service to pay our bills? There were many more questions touching on similar subjects. For the 20 years I had been in the aerospace field, I had received a pay check every week.

But this new work, which I had launched into, was different. There were no weekly pay checks as far as I could see. This was a new beginning, and I was scared.

I often prayed about the situation, for I had to know that what I was doing was really what God had planned for me. I needed to hear from God. And God answered, but not in the way I had expected.

One day I heard a tune playing over and over in my head. At first I didn't pay too much attention to it, but it stayed with me for a number of days. When it persisted, I decided to quiet myself and listen.

The melody was the familiar "Ol' Man River." Even though I heard it very clearly in my mind, I didn't know what it meant to me at that time. I asked Doris if she knew the words to that melody, and she reminded me of them. A few days later, as I kept going over the words to the song, the message became clear. "Don't worry over your concerns: Like Ol' Man River, just keep rolling along."

This was very encouraging. It told me to continue with what I was doing, and all my needs would be taken care of. I have found that to be so true. Over many years this guidance has proven to be right, and all our needs and more, have been met.

As Doris and I strive to follow God's guidance, our lives are enriched. It isn't always easy. There have been sacrifices and some painful experiences, but we've never been sorry. Following His guidance has consistently resulted in benefits to us, as well as to others. Besides, it has been a very exciting life.

Chapter 9

The Faceted Crystal

Like a ship rounding Cape Horn as it passes from the Atlantic Ocean to the Pacific, I have made headway in my spiritual voyage but not without some turbulent water. It has been akin to relocating from your comfortable home-town to another country. You enter your new life in a foreign land, excited by the adventures ahead and the promise of making new friends, but, as you exit the old home-town, regretfully, you leave behind cherished friends and treasured memories.

As God has revealed to me the steps of my spiritual development, and I have expanded my experience from Judaism to Christianity to counselor, sometimes I've had to surrender close ties with family and friends, as well as institutions and traditions. Not everyone has understood nor supported my journey. While I grieve over these losses, my convictions prevent compromise. I am committed to follow the path God has for me.

If I have one disappointment that looms above others, it is having to discontinue participating in traditional church activities. For so many years we enjoyed strong ties and loving fellowship in our church. Now, however, once my ideas on reincarnation and karma or my astral trips to the Akashic Records and intuitive readings are discovered, we are ostracized in most mainline churches. Yet I believe that these ideas are biblically sound and consistent with my fundamental Judeo-Christian beliefs.

It's like the anecdote about a group of people observing a column of light passing through a many-faceted crystal. As each one looks at the facet nearest him/her, each sees a slightly different color or hue. Some see a deep blue. Others, a light green. Still others insist the color is red or deep green.

51

Those who see nearly the same color become friends and start an organization for the preservation of the true color. For fear of being contaminated, they decline to converse with those who see different colors.

Quickly, more organizations are formed—one for every major color transmitted through the facets of the crystal, and many more for those who see the off-colored hues.

Each group believes the other groups have erred. Actually, they were all correct in their first perception. Depending upon which facet of the crystal they viewed, each saw a different color of light. Each believed that everyone else should have seen his/her color when actually each facet exhibits its own color.

What had started as a genuine search for the truth had turned into a dogmatic and unchanging group intent upon protecting its own truth.

Often the readings point out that truth is like a multi-faceted diamond—each facet represents a different aspect of truth or religious philosophy. Yet each facet is just a part of the same truth, only perceived from a different perspective.

Many aspects of religious practices and beliefs of others have been questioned by those who claim to have the only truth. However, we have come to believe that truth comes in many different colors, and that each color is part of the whole.

Consider astrology as one of the facets. The scriptures warn against its use although we know that in the Old Testament days, God gave astrology to the people for a tool to use as a means for guidance. They were instructed in

Genesis that the stars in the sky had been placed there for signs and seasons (Genesis 1:14). God placed a principle of guidance before them; it was their responsibility to find the proper use of it.

Also, the New English translation of the Bible says that the "wise men" who came from the East to see Jesus were astrologers (Matthew 2: 1-7). They used their knowledge of the stars to see a future event. Nowhere in these verses was it suggested that the practice was frowned upon. That's the way it is throughout the Bible. There are principles that when applied in a Godly and practical way will help bring guidance, order, and discipline into our lives.

God doesn't divulge everything. Much is left for us to figure out for ourselves and to discover realistic and practical solutions. Otherwise, where would our growth come from? If it were all done for us, we wouldn't learn.

It was only later when some self-serving people misused and abused the tools of astrology. That, I believe, is why the warning against such practices was given in the Old Testament. We have known some very fine astrologers in our day and times.

Whether astrology or divination, both are prohibited according to the Old Testament (Deuteronomy 18:10). Nevertheless, Jacob's son, Joseph, who occupied a prominent position in Egypt's government, used a divining cup. (Genesis 44:5). Yet is Joseph denounced? No. Nor do Bible scholars and ministers preach or teach against his use of the cup of divination. To this day Joseph is considered one of the most godly men in the Old Testament. He attributed all of his abilities to the work of God in and through him. We believe this is the key.

Most fundamental Christians lump the terms psyche, psychic, and mysticism together as being *from the devil.*

However, according to Webster's Dictionary, psyche means "the human mind, as in psychiatry, the mind is considered as an organic system reaching all parts of the body and serving to adjust the total organism to the needs or demands of the environment."

And psychic? "The activity which is beyond the natural or known physical processes." A dream, a vision, or revelation takes place within the psyche and is a psychic experience.

And mysticism simply means "doctrines or beliefs of mystics; specifically, the doctrine that it is possible to achieve communion with God through contemplation and love without the medium of human reason. Any doctrine that asserts the possibility of

53

attaining knowledge of spiritual truths through intuition acquired by fixed meditation."

It doesn't sound all that sinister.

Evelyn Underhill, in her book, "The Essentials of Mysticism," puts it very simple and direct. "Mysticism" she writes, "is union with reality." In this case reality is God.

Doris and I believe that when a Christian psychic uses his or her abilities as an instrument given by God to aid humanity, it is as honorable as Joseph's divining cup.

After all, nothing is evil or harmful about mysticism or astrology or the psyche unless we make it so. And we believe that neither is there anything contrary to the Bible's teaching as related to reincarnation.

Every Bible student remembers when the disciples questioned Jesus about Elijah and John the Baptist. They asked Jesus why the teachers of the law said that "Elijah must come first."

Jesus answered, "Elijah has already come and they didn't recognize him but have done to him everything they wished. Then the disciples understood that he was talking to them about John the Baptist" (Matthew 17:9-13). If their understanding was in error, it would seem that Jesus would correct them. He didn't.

On another occasion Jesus communicated with Moses and Elijah, both of whom had been dead many years (Mark 9:2-4). And Paul communicated with Jesus after He had already ascended into heaven (Acts 9:1-6).

Also, both Peter and Paul experienced a trance state (Acts 10:10; 22:17). There may have been more, but these are the only two that come to mind that are reported in the New Testament.

If we interpret the meaning of the words *psychic* and *psyche* correctly, we see that many of the unusual experiences in the Bible—which we call miracles, were actually psychic experiences. This doesn't make them any less miraculous, but it does lay a foundation for the many psychic experiences people have had since New Testament times. The use of the psyche is just an application of some of the laws of God, universal laws, established by God at the time of creation.

And when we compare the information received in the readings with the Bible, we are comfortable that there is no inconsistency with these sources of information and the principles of God as taught in both the Old and New Testaments.

The more facets of truth we recognize, the more we marvel at the greatness of God. It has lifted us into an ever-expanding awareness of the vastness of the love of God. Learning about these truths is exciting to us. Lessons from this side or the other side are always valuable teachers about ourselves and our relationships with God.

Chapter 10

Lessons from the Other Side

Shakespeare once said that the world is a stage, and everybody on it is an actor. Our readings often refer to life on Earth as a stage play. With its outcome depending on how seriously each player takes his/her role.

In a reading for a young woman who was trying to break into show business, she was reminded that everybody is special and that each person lends a unique talent to the performance. Without that particular contribution the play would lose some of its substance.

Naturally as it is in any play, not everybody can play the lead role. Neither can everyone make the costumes or direct the play, or work behind the scenes, or manage the public relations, nor sell tickets or do the work of the janitor.

It takes many people to produce a play. Each player needs to know the role assigned to him/her, and it is expected that all players put their hearts and souls into the performance; otherwise, the play may not be successful.

The reading told her that it is no different in the play taking place in life. Each of us has been given a specific part to play. A role that we have either selected or has been assigned to us prior to our present incarnation. Sometimes we even receive new role assignments within the same life period.

Whether or not our roles are as presidents of large corporations or as janitors in small companies isn't as important as how we carry out our responsibilities in those roles. Neither is it the position nor role in life that makes for a more meaningful journey. Rather, it is the positive attitudes and behaviors developed from the principles applied in these roles.

It was explained to her that through what we learn in these experiences, we can give hope to others and encourage them so that they can have an opportunity to grow and, in turn, help others. She was reminded that we will mature to the same degree that we kindly and caringly help others. The manner in which we are now carrying out the responsibilities in our roles in this life is important because it will also determine what we will do in future incarnations.

Another reading explained to 70 year old Jane that life doesn't just end one day. It continues on. Each time we return to this physical-material world, we may play a different role that is designed to help in our growth.

Perhaps in one life we may play the role of a very influential person or ruler, only to play the role in another lifetime of a servant in the house of a ruler. The reason for this is to give us a variety of experiences and some insight into the responsibilities, privileges, and duties of a number of life roles.

Information from the other side reminds us that when a soul is ready to enter another incarnation (and depending on its growth), it can choose the culture, family, and time to enter the physical plane again. If the soul hasn't shown the required growth and still desires to enter the physical plane, it is advised by its guides where, when, and at what time to enter.

These assigned guides will know what lessons the soul needs to learn before it has the knowledge and wisdom to move on to other areas of growth. So with this advice, the soul agrees and promises to do better. Then upon entering the physical realm, it finds itself in similar situations or circumstances as before and often with the same people. The experience is repeated in the hope that this time the soul will learn. We all know that repetition is one of the best ways to learn.

Much of what the soul goes through in one lifetime is a repetition of other life experiences. It may appear new because the culture, environment, language, and surroundings are different than the previous lifetimes.

A young man was told in a reading that the present situation is nothing new. He was urged to face each experience and work it out as well as he could so that he could learn the lessons better this time.

One lady wrote Doris and me that her life reading had done more for her than four years of psychological counseling. Though we are aware that those four years probably taught her how to recognize truths about herself, we're pleased that the information from the reading focused on her needs in such a way that she received immediate help. The reading had shed new light on her situation, and she felt she could cope better now and move on with her life.

Also, consider the teacher we mentioned in Chapter 3. She listened to her reading for five minutes and in disappointment put it away in a drawer. She didn't find it useful until ten years later. After many changes in her life, she listened to it again—this time to the end. She discovered that the profession she was now working in was what the reading had suggested for her life work.

More often people gain much help from their readings by listening to them a number of times over the following months and years. Obtaining a life reading is serious business. The information given is meant to be used as tools of understanding and as concepts about ourselves and our paths of life that help us in our present life. In this way it may be easier to recognize mistakes or misjudgments of the past, and present tendencies to similar responses are illuminated as our mind compares the present with the past. But how delightful it can be when comparison with the present reveals how much we've overcome and grown from the lessons of the past. Either way it is always helpful to know what areas of our lives need re-structuring.

John, a struggling businessman, was told in one reading that much of his difficulties stemmed from a lack of understanding about his priorities, which were not in the proper order for his best growth. The reading suggested that he rearrange his priorities with the top three always remaining the same. The top priority was to be his personal relationship with God. Second was to be his relationship and responsibility to his wife and then his children. The third was to be his relationship and commitment to his profession.

At the time of the reading, the third priority, his job, had been his first since he graduated from college. The reading explained that not only was it important to keep these three top priorities the same but also to keep them in the order they were given.

John was dismayed at first. His wife, Anita, urged him to try it before dismissing the suggestions. John was afraid that his work would suffer. Anita suggested that if his work began to suffer because of re-arranging his priorities, then he could always adjust his schedule.

It took some planning, rescheduling of time, and some reprogramming of thinking patterns, it worked. The result found him more secure as a person, happier in his marriage and family life, and more congenial and creative in his work.

In his report to us he wrote that in his working with the first priority, he found that the suggestions from the reading had been consistent with what he was discovering in his Bible reading. For instance, he said, in Matthew 6:33, he found, "Seek first the Kingdom of God and His righteousness and all these things will be added unto you." In another passage, he noted, "And you shall love the Lord your God with all your heart, all your might and all your mind, and love your neighbor as yourself." This presented to him a challenge that made his life more enriched and practical.

John was right, of course, for we are aware that principles such as these have not originated with the readings. We recognize them as having come down through the ages, carefully treasured in sacred writings.

A man, with similar concerns as John's, had been troubled with the thought that life ends when the physical body is laid to rest. In his reading it was stated that the process of life goes on and on. That in reality there is only one life. This life has always been and always will be. It has never had any beginning, nor will it have an end. In short, life *is*. Life is lived either in the physical or the non-physical worlds.

We are first spirit. In the physical life we clothe ourselves with a human body. When the physical, human body wears out or is damaged beyond repair, we leave it and continue on in our spirit body until we choose the next type of *clothing* to put on.

Within that one life there are many experiences that include the birth and death encounter. Birth does not mean a beginning; neither does death mean an end. It is only a continuance of what has been before. Life is a process of going from one physical experience to a non-physical experience, then back to the physical experience, and on and on and on.

To understand life, the counsel went on to say that it is helpful to be aware that life is what each person, as spirit-being, experiences on this as well as other planes, that life can be experienced whether in the physical or non-physical state. But the reading also reminded him that there is a saying that life is not meant to be a problem to be solved, but an experience to be lived. In that experience, some events bring joy and some sorrow. But regardless, we can remain a happy person if we are at peace with ourselves and with God.

The need for happiness is seen in so many requests we receive, and we wish we had a secret formula, which would produce instant happiness. We don't have such a recipe. So many think that wealth will bring happiness, but the readings echo what wise men of old have said, that wealth will not make you happy. It can, of course, give you a more comfortable life, and let's face it, there is nothing wrong with that. But there can be more.

Some people believe that meeting their soul mate will make them happy. A number of letters that has come to us indicate this. But even that does not guarantee happiness.

One reading started by saying that life, of it's self, can't make us happy. We must learn to BE a happy person in order to HAVE a happy life. Challenges and difficulties, sorrows and pain, love and joy are all part of life. That is what is involved with life. The difficulty and pain are sacrifices we make, the lessons we learn from them are our rewards, and love and joy are the bonuses.

Through these lessons we learn that much of life is involved with preparing ourselves for continued growth, for taking action on what we believe, and for expecting favorable results.

If we are a happy person, life will be a happy experience, regardless of the circumstances and/or the environment in which we live. If we are not a happy person, no amount of good things in our life will make us happy. The good things might make life more pleasant but not necessarily more happy. The bottom line in any life is to grow into maturity. Following the three top priorities will make this possible.

A young woman asked if there might be a map that she could follow to help her grow spiritually. She had tried many methods and searched in many places. She wanted something she could hold onto. The information obtained in the reading was not surprising.

It explained that within each soul there is a seed from God which, when unfolded, will reveal a map by which the soul is to travel. Usually only one step at a time is revealed. This map will bring into consciousness the purpose of the soul, the path it should follow, and the karma it has to meet.

With each karma we meet, we are constantly making contact with ourselves. As often as we try to avoid meeting our karma, we are really just avoiding meeting ourselves and delaying the growth that can be ours. However, the karma will continue to surface until the time comes when we will eventually see the futility of running away from ourselves and begin to change our karmic patterns.

This change can be a rewarding experience through which we will have the opportunity to learn about ourselves and grow. The young women was cautioned not to be discouraged by any obstacles or difficulties encountered in working through her karma, for she would soon recognize this karma as a stepping stone to further spiritual growth and understanding. Further advice urged her not to pursue her karmic responsibilities too vigorously, lest she become insensitive to others in the process and build several new karmas while resolving the old one.

In addition, the information supplied further amplification to the process of growth. While in the process of resolving these karmic patterns and learning to live with ourselves, it was pointed out that there is a continual tutoring taking place between the spirit and the soul.

The spirit, thought by some to be the super-conscious mind, imparts to the soul, or the sub-conscious mind, what it desires to be impressed upon the conscious mind. This is in the form of suggestions and seed thoughts only and often as little gems of truth, not in *hard fast* commands. The soul has the responsibility of choosing what lessons it will bring to the attention of the conscious mind, such as how he/she should respond to his/her many experiences in order to become aware of how to set in proper order the priorities that the conscious mind needs to address. Through this method, several options are presented to the individual from which he can choose the one to his best liking at that moment.

For every subject the conscious mind shows an interest in, there is always a ready input from the spirit to the soul. Hopefully the soul will understand the instructions from the spirit and direct them to the conscious mind.

This doesn't mean that the individual becomes a robot or that all decisions are made for him/her. The individual is still a free agent. He/she can take the advice offered or completely ignore it.

No matter how the individual responds to the counsel, the result is transmitted to the soul who compares it with the suggestions offered. In turn, the soul relays its findings to the spirit who compares the end result with the truth given. Questions arise. How persuasive was the soul in making the suggestions to the conscious mind, and how well did the individual respond so that the purpose of God could be carried out?

The soul, acting as a go-between for the spirit and the conscious mind, may not always be in accord with the spirit. If the soul becomes rebellious, it may block the input from the spirit, thus relaying distorted information to the conscious mind. The reading pointed out this is why a person needs to feed his/her minds, soul, and spirit through reading and studying spiritual material that will inspire him/her. In addition he/she needs to pray and meditate on a daily basis and work to integrate all levels of himself/herself mentally, spiritually, emotionally, and physically.

Therefore, the readings go on to say, that over a period of many lifetimes the soul will eventually hear clearly the message from the spirit, and with patience, it will continue to impress it upon the conscious mind until the individual lovingly responds to the desires of the spirit. At that point there will be unity on all levels of self and peace between the soul and spirit.

In this way the individual writes his/her own ticket for the number of return trips he/she will make to planet Earth to resolve what is required before she is free of the need to learn through the physical body and be allowed to move on. In the words of the Master, "You shall know the truth, and the truth shall make you free."

The bottom line of all this is that each individual is responsible for all of his/her actions. So it is important to take the opportunity to grow from the resulting experiences.

Many years ago we heard the phrase, "When the student is ready, the teacher will appear." To us, this meant that when we had matured enough, a physical teacher would knock on our door one day and start to teach us. Sometimes it could be just that. Like when a Bible teacher came to our home and taught us in a personal way about the Bible. These teaching sessions lasted for many months, and we are grateful for this teacher who made herself available to us.

But more often, the teacher appears in a different way.

The readings remind us that everything in life is meant to be a learning experience. Any experience, especially those that involve relationships with family and friends or colleagues at the workplace, can be an opportunity for learning, an opportunity to apply the principles we have discovered, an opportunity to listen and hear, and an opportunity to be a more caring person. As we become aware of the opportunity to learn from everything in life, we make ourselves ready to recognize the teacher inherent in the experience. Learning and growing in knowledge and awareness is an ongoing process. We never learn it all in one lifetime.

There are still those who ask us to find a guru for them. They are serious about their growth and are eager to find the one who can teach them what they need. One reading put it this way, "That the guru is closer than they realize! In each experience they have gone through, the guru has been in that adventure. The teacher has been there all the time, but will not be recognized until the student is ready and open to the lesson inherent in the experience. Therefore, we may consider the experience itself as the teacher." The readings say that the time of the guru as such, the teacher who will take responsibility for us and make decisions for us, is over. It is time to take responsibility for our own actions.

We can experience plateaus and resting places, but if we stand still too long, we start losing ground, for a person is either moving forward or backward. For this very reason, it is important for all of us to realize that since life is a growing adventure and a journey of change, the effort we make to apply what we know to be right for us should result in a growing and more meaningful experience. Teachers are still important, for they can point the way, inspire and motivate us. The readings just urge us to take responsibility for our own actions and for our own growth, especially as we approach the end of this time span and go beyond.

Each life is an experience consisting of many events from which we can build a better understanding of why we are here.

When some of the events we go through become quite difficult, it can be very perplexing and discouraging, and we wonder why.

A man in his 40's wrote us asking why all these things happened to him? So many ordeals had taken place in his life. He wanted to know if it would ever change?

Yes, the reading assured him. Change is something we can count on. Nothing remains the same forever. Those who have faced difficult and painful encounters over and over again may feel that their difficulties will last forever, but they won't. Change is always on the horizon of hope but not fully realized until we begin to understand the importance each experience should have in our life. Then, upon grasping the lessons discerned in the experiences and beginning to practice the principles found, change is at last inevitable.

Finally, we may have recognized the need to initiate the changes ourselves—in ourselves and/or in our situations. More often, the inner changes we make will result in outer changes, thus effecting a change in our situation.

Each experience can be a signpost to tell us how we are progressing. If we are teachable, intuitively alert and sensitive, we may begin to recognize the message the experience brings and listen to what it says. But not all of us can see this message the first time around. As similar situations face us again and again, we may finally wake up to the truth of what the experience is telling us.

As we begin to hear the message from the depths of our souls, we will experience a change in our outlook. Practicing the principles from the lesson learned in each experience is one of the quickest and most effective ways to grow and progress in our spiritual and physical life. If we didn't hear the message the first time, the teacher will present a variety of encounters for us. All of these encounters represent the same lessons in many different forms and settings.

The many experiences we meet in our daily life are like an attorney pleading his case before a jury. His responsibility is to bring before the members of the jury many different views of the case being tried until they fully understand the situation. Finally, the jury must weigh the evidence and decide. And we are the jury.

It is up to us to consider the issues in our situation, and determine what the message is or what the lesson is that we are to learn. The decision will emerge as we begin to listen to the many various challenges we meet each day.

It doesn't matter how many experiences we go through in a lifetime. What matters is what we are learning from these events as we recognize the message. The experience can be compared to a loaded freight car. What it carries—the substance—is what's important. What matters even more is that we take some form of positive action based on the lesson.

A man in his 70's was still holding resentment towards his deceased father for giving more attention to his older brother when they were growing up. By the response to such a person, time and again, the information in the readings reminds us to learn to give thanks for everything that happens to us. Difficult as that is, giving thanks to God for the situation will help us obtain another perspective on the problems and enable us to get a better look at what we are going through. That understanding will help us grow. This concept is not original with the readings. The Bible also teaches it.

Then the reading went on to urge him to learn to forgive his father and brother and release the resentment he felt toward them. Though this is always a painful lesson and difficult to apply, when the effort is made to do it, it becomes a quick and effective way to grow and learn.

All of us have been hurt by someone to some degree, the readings remind us. We all have been intimidated, ignored, rejected, abused, or opposed by someone. Through all this, we have tried to ignore it and tell ourselves it doesn't matter—when it really does. We have been hurting, sometimes for many years, and all that hurt has been pushed down inside where it has festered and caused great harm. This can result in damage to our physical and emotional states. Resentment will build a fortress within us that affects the normal functioning of our body and mind. It can also present a block to our spiritual growth.

Then if we would take the time to forgive those who have hurt us, we will begin to feel the power of release. Forgiving others is just as helpful to us, as it is to the other person. Forgiving is NOT approving of what was done.

The process of forgiving can be very simple. Just visualize those who have caused the distress in our life, even if some are deceased. Then mention each person by name and say, "I forgive you." It may be necessary to continue with this until we have covered everyone who has had a negative influence in our life. We need to repeat this as often as it is necessary until we know that we have truly forgiven. The completion of this process may take months or years. Regardless of how long it takes, the readings encourage us to continue to forgive for as long and as often as needed.

We need also to forgive ourselves for allowing others to hurt us and vent their negativity on us, and for the things we have done that have hurt others. Of course, the readings tell us, it is just as important for us to ask those whom we have hurt to forgive us.

It matters little whether those whom we forgive are in the physical or non-physical worlds—the benefit is the same. Many are still suffering from the results of resentment toward family members and friends who have already made the transition from this plane to the next one. The same method of forgiving is as effective in these cases.

In one reading an athlete was told that life is like a race that has an obstacle course. Thus, we are the only ones in our own races. The readings often say that if we just keep doing our best and never give up, we will win the race.

A lady told us that she had studied metaphysics all her adult life and that she meditates for two hours every day at the same time in the afternoon. She complained that now that her husband had retired she gets so angry at him because he interrupts her during her meditation period. She was planning to chase him out of the house during those two hours.

Her reading began with a long discourse on the importance of applying knowledge. As we pursue life, we accumulate knowledge. If this accumulation knowledge is never used except to decorate our intellect, then that information is useless to us and we have wasted our time.

The principles found in knowledge are there for us to apply. Whether they are gleaned from periods of meditation or reading and studying, their application to our life will enable us to handle the daily irritations in a more loving way. If we're not coping more lovingly, it is because we aren't applying the principles we find from knowledge. It is better to read and study very little and apply much than to read a great deal and apply little.

As we apply the principles to the best of our understanding, wisdom will eventually emerge. And we will discover that our life is improving. Our life will become more meaningful as we dare to accept the possibility that we have a limited viewpoint and find room within ourselves to go beyond what earlier was unacceptable, therefore breaking through the barriers of that limitation.

The reading went on to say that the pathway to spiritual growth does not come by observation alone; neither does it come only by intellectual acknowledgment. Though both are important, it also requires from us consistent effort, dedication and commitment. Time after time our purpose will surface on the sea of accomplishments or failures. Each time it will remind us of our intent. Therefore, never become discouraged. Never give up. Never allow failures to crowd out dreams. Never allow successes to go to your head. Instead, direct them to your hearts. And always we need to keep in mind what our purpose is, no matter what the circumstances are. Doing this, provides a compass by which we can discern our direction when we are confronted with choices.

A young man wrote that he felt it would help him so much if he could know what his purpose in life was. He described himself as only an auto mechanic, but felt that his purpose was something special. However, it seemed to him that he was just treading water.

According to his letter to us later, his reading put many things in the proper perspective, and having seen this life in a broader scope, he was more content. His real purpose, the reading pointed out, was to be a spiritual mechanic by bringing people together in groups so they could learn to work as a unit. This would be much like putting together the automotive parts so the engine could function well.

His reading indicated that he had great talent for the field in which he was working, but because his work was so easy for him, he had not recognized that his abilities were special, nor had he realized that he might apply this ability in a special way.

There is no one purpose that's more important than another, the reading continued. All are important. All purposes are special, but we will have to supply that special ingredient to make it so. It doesn't matter who we are or what we are, whether the President, janitor, minister, teacher, student, or whatever. What matters is what attitudes are practiced in carrying out that purpose. It is the substance in our life that helps to provide that special ingredient. The position we hold in this present life is not what makes us a person of substance but the attitudes and motives we cultivate in our daily life.

So we can ask ourselves, suggested the reading, "What is the purpose of life? What is the purpose of a nation? What is the purpose of the world?" The general answer is quite simple: to learn, to grow, to mature, and ,of course, to help and encourage one another. For whether we live in crowded conditions or pleasant circumstances or work under hardships or blessings, that doesn't excuse us from trying to learn and to grow. Some of this learning comes by reflecting upon the past and combining it with the present. This may help us make better decisions for the present and future. Our purpose may have very little or nothing to do with our profession or career, but the one can always help the other in some way.

"The journey to maturity," the reading went on, "involves our attitudes and motives. These are important in the growth of a soul. The motives are the guiding factors in our growth. In the long run, the motives build the attitudes. This is the cement that molds our character, dignity, and integrity. Without the proper motives it is difficult, if not impossible, to live honestly in this world. And without honest attitudes, one can't make the proper responses to life.

"As we go through life, we need to be caring and of service to those around us. If in our entire life we have helped only one person by giving hope and encouragement, we may consider ourselves very successful."

The inscription over the entrance to the Oracle of Delphi reads: "Know Thyself." This has been a subject that has also been addressed in the readings, and the information from the other side has brought out some helpful thoughts.

For instance, one reading pointed out that knowing ourselves is the product of a long, often difficult process called integration. Integration can be a goal, but it may be wise to keep our eye on the process of integration and allow that process to be part of the goal.

The process of integration is a necessary one, the readings urged. Here we can begin to confront ourselves on many levels (mental, emotional, spiritual and physical) and under many different circumstances. In bringing all aspects of ourselves together, there can be unity and harmony. The process of integration can sometimes cause friction and turbulence, but it is a worthwhile process. It should result in a rebirth of a new personality and mentality, as well as a new insight into the intellectual and spiritual paths of our lives.

The reading went on to explain that it is best to begin with where we are at the present moment. We need to learn to be honest with ourselves and learn to love ourselves for who we are. As we work with what is at hand, we can be observant and listen to the still small voice from within. As we face each situation, we reach into our mental, spiritual, emotional, and physical selves and blend all the understanding from these. Then we respond to the situation from that integrated viewpoint. In doing this, we will begin to recognize, little by little, that we are growing.

The universal truth about any growth in the spiritual realm is that it takes one step at a time, one truth at a time. Yet, there is only one truth. So it is helpful to understand that it is usually one facet of the truth at a time. For the entire truth consists of many facets; it comes in many colors, packages and shapes; and travels in many different directions.

Such information reveals to us that depending upon which direction is chosen, one may pursue one path while another follows a different approach. We are reminded of the well worn words of Thoreau that seems to apply here: "If a man does not keep pace with his companions, perhaps it is because he hears a different drummer. Let him step to the music which he hears, however measured or far away." These words may seem trite, but they are truth.

The readings remind us that the many paths of truth will eventually merge, and then a greater part of the truth will be seen and understood for what it is. Because a facet of truth is deposited within each soul, each can learn from the other. So if all people desire to know more of the truth, they need to cooperate with each other and listen to the truth each person has.

The merging of many paths, or many facets of the truth, will mean there will eventually be more harmony and agreement in the world. This may finally lead to peace on Earth.

"Peace," the information continues, "is what everyone is searching for, and in this search there must come eventually a realization that it originates with the Prince of Peace. Therefore, in this pursuit it is helpful to begin to understand oneself in relationship to God, so that there can be a more wholesome expression of oneness among all people.

"When there is unity and peace in our personal world and as we influence others for good, there can be peace in their worlds, also. Hopefully, this chain reaction can continue until all people can experience and live in peace. Through this method, there can eventually be peace in the entire world." It has been said that there really is no way to peace—that peace is the way.

However, the readings point out that peace must exist first within each person; true peace can't be legislated. It has to be experienced in the hearts of the people and lived out through their behavior. When a person has storms and turbulence raging within, it becomes very difficult, if not impossible, to think or behave in a manner of true peace. Nor can that person be a very effective initiator of true peace.

All in all, we are promised in the readings, that we can make the living of our lives an enjoyable expression. We are reminded of how exciting learning can be; and how rewarding it is to bring hope and encouragement to others. In so doing, our lives are never boring or uninteresting. If we can learn a little and apply it well in just one lifetime, we have done well. In addition, the readings remind us that the Universe and the world are dependent upon our willingness to learn and grow.

Chapter 11

A Symphony in Music and Color

Through the years many subjects have come through the readings, and all of them have increased our interest in wanting to know all we possibly can. But there is one topic that has intrigued us and one that we wish we had more time to explore. That subject is music and color and their effects on all levels of the human environment.

Our personal experience with this subject came as a surprise for us, but one we long remember. Some years ago when we were living in San Diego, the interior of our home needed to be repainted. We decided to do the living room in a powder blue. After its completion, we noticed how good we felt when we allowed the blue color to wrap itself around us, and we started to realize the healing effect this color had on our bodies, as well as on our mental and emotional states. From that time on, we started to become sensitive to the colors we would have around us, especially in our home and in our clothing.

Several years later a friend of ours, who was a nurse on the psychiatric ward in the local hospital, told us that the hospital administrator in a memo had said that the nurses no longer needed to wear white uniforms. They could use whatever color clothing they liked.

Our friend then asked if I could do a reading for her in regards to what colors would be best for her to use in her work place, to act as a catalyst for the healing of her patients.

The information from the reading went a step further. It gave her what colors to wear each day, Monday through Friday, and further explained the rationale behind it.

"There are a few colors which are predominantly good for healing, and we have healing, now, in two aspects—namely in the physical and in the spiritual. Now when she appears in that particular part of the hospital where she is now engaged, keep in mind, that which we are now giving need not be followed explicitly, but these are only examples that we are putting forth."

The reading gives information as to what colors this person could wear for each day. On Monday, lavender is suggested, for this color is both quieting and uplifting as well as being inspiring. Because Monday is the first day of her week, something of inspirational value needs to be used in order to get the week started in the right direction. The lavender is the color needed to bring these influences to those in her work place, as well as for her own well being.

On Tuesday, the reading went on, she could wear green. For a point of reference, this color relates to the soil and the healing of the whole being. This color can be between grass green and emerald green. Sometimes the darker greens, like forest green, can be used, but use discernment as to when to wear the darker colors.

The color orange, which is good for the emotional body and will start it functioning, can be used on Wednesday, the reading suggests. The orange color can also be toned down into the pink shades with good results for the healing of the emotional body. But at the same time the pink color will also be very quieting for the person. On Thursday, wear yellow, the reading goes on, in as much as yellow appeals to the healing of the mind. Then on Friday, repeat the lavender used on Monday for the calming and spiritual healing of the people.

When Saturday comes along, the reading states, wear green again for that will connect you with the soil, and healing for your own body can take place. Then on Sunday, wear blue to relax the body, mind, and spirit, and to properly prepare you for the next week.

There appeared to be a progression in attitudes, effectiveness in service and growth during the week in the use of the colors suggested. The nurse reported that the benefit of the colors

76

suggested in the reading was of great benefit to her, as well as those on the psychiatric ward.

She felt more at peace with herself and the world around her, and was able to handle stressful situations much better than previously. Another benefit from the use of these colors was that she was able to be a better nurse with a clearer understanding of daily situations that allowed her to make better decisions with peace of mind.

The information from the reading also suggested that the colors to be used should be very distinct as to the color and shade, but no sharp colors, otherwise it would disturb those on the ward. The colors should be clear enough so those who are exposed to them can experience the healing powers of these colors.

The application of the suggestions from this one reading made us more interested in looking into what would be the effects of color on the spiritual, mental, and physical bodies. We decided to do a whole series of readings on color. While planning those sessions, we felt that there might be a connection between color and music; thus it was decided to do a series of readings on music, also.

In February 1972, the first reading in the series on color was taken. The information started with the color red and gave the effects of red when used in daily life. For example, the reading stated that the color red can be dangerous and yet uplifting, depending upon who uses it and at what times. It also stated that this color is identified with the middle C on the piano. This color which is very strong, is an emotional color, and also a color for service. Red is a color that brings both health and destruction, good and bad, weak and strong. Frustrations and disappointments are also associated with this color, as well as hope and glory. This color appears to be one of extremes, and if not used with discernment, it can produce a radical change in the behavior of a person and eventually make him hyperactive. These changes can be very subtle, and not readily discovered.

This was brought out several years later in a reading for a young woman. The reading gave the information she needed to hear, but there was also a section on what color to avoid for her own well being. That color was red. The reading even went so far as to warn her against the use of the color red because it would only agitate her and make a bad situation worse.

Sometime later she came to visit us, and both Doris and I could easily see how high-strung she was. Then she remarked that she didn't like that part of the reading where it spoke of avoiding the color red. She said that she had red all through her house, including the bedroom. She said she could see where that color could make her high-strung, but she liked the color and wasn't sure if she was willing to change it to another color that would be more beneficial for her. That was the last contact we had with her.

But we have also found some benefits from the use of this color. Whenever we feel in need of some extra physical energy, we wear a garment with red in it, but not for too long. We became alert to the fact that a little of this color is greatly beneficial, but wearing it too long can become detrimental to our well being.

In April of 1972, a reading on the color orange was done. This was followed by readings on the remaining colors. The reading said that orange is both a stimulating and quieting color. It stimulates the body for the healing process to take place, and it has a quieting effect upon the ailments. This color, according to the reading, corresponds to the note D, above middle C, on the piano.

The color pink, according to the information from the readings, could act as an incubator, a stabilizer and a confidant for the physical, emotional, intellectual, and spiritual facets of the human individual.

Pink is good for the healing of the heart on the emotional, physical and spiritual levels. The healing of the intellectual is also affected, making the intellect flexible, instead of maintaining a rigid attitude.

The yellow color would affect the mind, the intellect, and the healing of the same. It is very effective in bringing into balance the functioning of many of the systems in the physical/spiritual body, thus bringing about a better form of integration. Because of the benefit of pink on the intellect, both pink and yellow can be used at the same time.

The color blue would help in strengthening the will power. The readings suggest that those who have a weak will, would do well to use some garments of cobalt or royal blue. After awhile, changes for a better internal environment can begin to be experienced. The lighter colors, like powder blue, will help to take the sharp edges off the extremely strong and adamant will. If very much of the deeper color is used, it is suggested that there be accents of white or other pale colors.

When the colors lavender and purple are used with discretion, they will act as a catalyst for spiritual growth. However, if the dark colors are overused or used unwisely, it could induce depression or unexplained sadness.

The readings suggest that some experimentation be used to find out what colors would be suited for each person. We need to develop and use our own intuition and discover how the body is working and responding to the colors.

Music therapy has also been dealt with in the readings, and much helpful information has been obtained. The readings give a list of what musical instruments would be best for therapy, and the first one is the harp, followed by the violin and piano played together. The third one would be the piano by itself, then the flute, the guitar, the clarinet, and the French horn. The instruments for music therapy must have rich, full sound that will produce a harmonious vibration and good resonance. The cello will produce these qualities, and it is an excellent instrument for the healing of the body.

The readings state that for the most part classical music should be used for therapy, such selections as the Grand Canyon Suite, Beethoven's Moonlight Sonata and his symphonies, the

79

Gregorian chants, especially those which are composed by Palestrina, Grieg's piano concerto, Bach, Handel and Hayden are also included as is the music by Mozart. There is also a whole range of folk music from Italy and the operas by Verdi. There is also the temple music from Japan, Hebrew melodies, French music, and compositions from Wagner and Schubert. There are many more composers included in the list, but the above selections can serve as a start.

The readings go on to state that music and color therapy is an art, and as such, it must be practiced if we are to learn it. But it can only be effectively administered by those who are intuitive themselves.

The information from the readings gives a good reason for music and color therapy. It is better called attunement of body, soul, and spirit. As the musician needs to tune his instrument prior to a rehearsal, so must the physical body likewise be tuned before it can operate at its optimum level. In that respect the physical body is much like a musical instrument. When it is tuned right, it will be able to see beyond its physical senses.

It is important to understand that every fiber within the physical body needs to be held in alignment so as to be attuned to the very high vibrations of the Universe. Keep now in mind that as the strings are to the violin, so is the spine to the physical body. For when one string is missing, the violin can still be played by a master but with some limitations. And though some of the vertebras may be out of alignment, the physical body can still function but in a limited degree.

Each vertebra is attuned to a very specific frequency. For example, the very lowest vertebra, starting now at the bottom, is attuned to "C" while the highest, the one that is closest to the neck or to the brain stem, is attuned to a "B"-natural. So there is a whole range of musical notes to which each vertebra is attuned. The first nine vertebras are on a nine note musical scale, and after that they are on a seven note scale. The vertebras can be attuned by applying the vibrations of a tuning fork directly to the vertebras, with each vertebra receiving its own natural frequency. The quality of healing for the spine will be very effective when the spine is able to function in a more proper way.

However, if the entire spine could be subjected to the note of "A"-natural, starting at the top and move toward the bottom, that would be a uniform or universal note for the entire single cord. This would be the most effective means for a quick indication of healing of the spine, but if each vertebra could be attuned to its own natural frequency, that would be much more effective.

In another reading, information concerning the soul and its vibratory state was given as follows: "Each soul is tuned to a particular frequency in the same manner as a musician would tune his instrument to a specific note. For within the soul's structure there are three specific frequencies to which the soul will vibrate: body, mind and spirit. But the highest of all these vibrations is that of your spiritual identity, which is concerned with spiritual goals, spiritual attainment, and spiritual progress. This is the vibration that is common to all souls.

"As the soul continues to vibrate, and responds to the vibrations of other souls, so can there be harmony among all souls and the development of a musical composition—namely the music of the Universe, the music of the Ages. And this is a composition the soul is capable of developing within itself."

The information from the readings state that music and color are like tools in the hands of a craftsman. This tool is not to be used indiscriminately. As a craftsman who would build a house wouldn't use dynamite that would destroy his work, so it is with color and music. We must learn how to use this tool as one would learn to walk, read, and write.

Then the readings give some information about what colors to use for general healing: emerald to grass green for the internal organs, orange to pink for the heart, lavender for the rest of the organs, golden yellow for the legs, blue for the thyroid and the thymus, and again lavender/purple for the mind and the brain.

To experiment with music and color, one reading stated, that it would be helpful if a room could be set aside for music and color sessions, though that would not be necessary, only helpful. The ideal shape of the room would be circular, painted white, with white drapes and carpet. If at all possible, a domed ceiling would be helpful. The reason for this is that the vibrations and the resonances will be transmitted much better and with more ease, so the person in the room would find that he/she was in the center of and surrounded by the music and color activity.

In our experience, we have discovered that almost any room can be converted into a circular room for music and color healing. White sheets were hung from a circular track in the ceiling, and the floor was covered with an inexpensive white carpet. On the outside of the draped sheets, four fixtures, each containing three lights in the primary colors, were placed equidistant around the circular track in the ceiling. Each colored light was operated through a dimmer switch so that the brightness of light could be controlled. In this manner the colors could also be mixed to obtain a spectrum of colors and shades. The white sheets and carpet would take on the color used; if pink were used, the entire healing room became pink; if yellow were used, it would become yellow, and so on.

A practical demonstration of color and music attunement with dramatic results was seen some years ago at one of our conferences in Montana.

A young man, out on probation, came to hear Dr. Maria De Rungs' lecture on music and color healing. Afterwards he showed an interest in the subject and asked if he could experience a music and color session. For the conference, a small silo had been converted for the music and color attunement sessions. After just one 30 minute session, the young man said he felt better in every way, and then he left.

A few weeks later, Dr. De Rungs received a letter from the young man's parole officer who related to her that he had seen such a significant change for the better over this young man that he wondered what she had done to him. She wrote him back and told him what therapy she had used with music and color. There was no reply from the parole officer.

We met Maria DE Rungs in 1972 when we lived in Oregon. She was then a music teacher and a professional cellist. She became interested in using music and color for the purpose of healing and studied our readings relating to that subject. She edited our music and color readings, and we placed the information in a booklet called "Attunement of Body, Soul and Spirit through Music and Color." She later left her University teaching position and started a research center (Casa DE Maria Research Center) in Everett, Washington, to research the healing effects music and color has on the physical body. She has used our readings as a basis for her research. In her work some remarkable results have come to light. (She is now retired.)

Judith, age 26, had Hodgkin's disease. She had refused medicine and chemotherapy treatments. From November 28,1984, to March 21, 1985, she had weekly sessions consisting of music from Bach, Beethoven, Chopin and Mendelssohn, with the colors appropriate for the music. Before the music sessions started her white blood count was far outbalancing the red count. Her blood pressure was very low, and the lymphatic system exhibited blockages. There were difficulties in her nervous and glandular systems. At the conclusion of her last session, all her difficulties had been cleared up with the result that the coloring of her skin was better, her swollen liver was reduced, the film over her eyes had disappeared, her sleep pattern and temperature had stabilized, and the digestive system was greatly improved.

The music from Bach helped repair the neurological system, making it more in harmony with the brain function. Beethoven's compositions worked with the mental processes and the energy field to re-establish normal harmony. The vibrations from Chopin's music worked to unblock the lymphatic and glandular systems. Mendelssohn's music worked on the energy system of

83

the heart, allowing the healing to be regenerated throughout the body.

Kali, age 2, had been suffering from fear. After just one session with Wagner's prelude to Parsifal, she was greatly improved. She had been ill for three weeks and was clinging to her mother in a fearful state. Both mother and child participated in the session. The music was played while both were lying down, stomach to stomach, in the attunement room. A polarity treatment was also given at this time. A few moments into the session the child relaxed and fell asleep. When she awakened, she was peaceful and gave the therapist a hug. The next day her mother reported that Kali was again her happy self, able to laugh and play.

Frank was suffering from a mental disorder. He had experienced tremendous fear and said he often heard people talking and knew that they were planning to kill him. He also heard voices when no one was present.

He was given music and color sessions three times a week for three months. As those progressed he was given counseling for his attitudes and emotions and nutritional deficiencies. The music sessions consisted of a prelude of Wagner's music drama, Tannhauser or Lohengrin, and selections of Schubert's Lieder. Yellow light was used to bring him joy and helped strengthen his determination to overcome his fear.

At the end of the sessions, he took charge of his healing process with strength and determination. The music, color, and improved nutrition were tools that he used to create a condition of harmony where there had been none.

Jody, age 24, a very capable and intelligent woman had no desire to work. This condition had gone on for a year when she came to the research center for help. She received music and color therapy once a week for two months. The music was Bach's Brandenburg Concerto No. 2, which was followed by ten minutes of Gregorian chants.

The Bach music worked to balance the emotional and mental energies while the Gregorian chants helped with her spiritual uplifting by bringing direction in her life. The combination of these two types of music brought focus and perspective to her life. At the conclusion of the session, Jody obtained a job and was able to interact with her co-workers.

It should be understood that no part of this material is presented as sectarian teachings or as cures or prescriptions for the treatment of diseases. It should be kept in mind that the suggestions in this material could be more of a projection into the far future in regards to the properties of color and music. We are not to be held responsible for anything that may occur as a result of experimenting with the information in this material. If a person suffers from illness, the family physician should be consulted.

Chapter 12

From the Edge of Light

So far, it's been a marvelous journey. Doris and I have participated in an interesting, educational, and enlightening experience. Some of the lessons we have learned in this life have been easy, fun and pleasant; others have been difficult, painful and stressful. Yet we know that our life experiences have not been that much different from anyone else's. We have learned from it all, and we are still learning.

Like others, during one period in our lives, we boxed ourselves in very tightly. But little by little we've managed to expand the sides of our box and today breathe more easily. We see a little farther than before. Our area of understanding has broadened, and our capacity for knowledge, deepened. We have gained an appreciation for wisdom and remain convinced that any wisdom we acquired and shared is a result of answered prayers—ours and others.

And we are grateful for our Judeo-Christian foundation—that substructure that opened our eyes to the mysteries of God, and girds us for further growth and experiences.

We stand ready to walk through the next door and/or to climb toward the next level in our spiritual development. And even if we should come to the "edge of all the light we have," seeing nothing but darkness ahead, we have faith that when we take the next step, we will either find "something solid for us to stand on—or we'll be taught how to fly." (Quotes by Claire Norris)

And the process continues.

Earthquakes,

Pole Shift

and

Survival

<u>**Text in bold print is a direct quote
from the readings**</u>

Chapter 13

EARTH CHANGES

I was awakened by loud creaking and groaning, sounds so unfamiliar that fear engulfed my being. The bed shook and rolled across the floor. Instantly, I was wide awake. Lea ping out of bed, I tried to walk into the living room but only managed to turn in circles. I yelled hysterically to Doris, "Let's get out of here!"

Our second floor apartment in South Pasadena, California, rocked like a ship in heavy sea, and being a Navy veteran, I was quite familiar with the rolling motions of ships at sea. But I was not aboard a sea-going vessel, yet the motion of the apartment building told a different story. It was, indeed, rolling like a ship in heavy seas.

Earthquake! Neither of us had experienced anything like this before. Needless to say, we were frightened and felt quite helpless. It was 4 A.M., July 21, 1952. This was the Tehachapi earthquake with a magnitude of 7.7 on the Richter scale. According to the periodical "United States Earthquakes," it was the largest earthquake in the U.S. since 1906.

Some years later while we were living in Big Bear Lake, East of Los Angeles, a friend told us of seeing a Public Broadcasting TV program on which scientists were discussing earthquakes. One of the panelists explained that an area under the Los Angeles basin from the coastal shelf and inland to the foot of the mountains was structured like a honeycomb. Therefore, he suggested that in a severe quake situation it would be possible

91

that whole sections would crumble, leaving no support for the land above it. Though the scientists would give no dates for such a catastrophe, they still concluded that a devastating earthquake was overdue in California. Some suggested it could happen sometime in the next 20 years.

After we discovered I could obtain information from the Akashic Records, in early 1971 we decided to take a reading to see if we could get some detailed information on earthquakes. We recognize now that the information we received then about these changes and our conclusions may appear to be unrealistic. Nevertheless, we hope that this information will be read with an open mind, and consideration will be given to the concepts and possibilities presented here.

The first reading was taken while we were living in Santa Maria, California. This first experience in doing readings on Earth changes convinced us that we didn't have sufficient knowledge on the subject matter to ask intelligent questions. Then after we had moved to Oregon, a geologist whom we knew, discussed the matter with us and offered to assist in forming more intelligent questions.

He had studied the Edgar Cayce readings and was hoping to obtain more information on the subject. He was so interested in the project that he offered to come to Oregon with his tectonic, geological, and shaded relief maps and help in the development of the readings.

We were delighted to have help from an expert such as he, and in 1972 gratefully invited him to stay with us while this series of readings was developed.

During the taping sessions as I gave the readings, the geologist sat on the floor surrounded by his open maps. As the information was given, he scanned the maps and often asked further questions for clarification. From time to time he was directed to make certain marks on the maps, like lines or circles. Even though Aron had his eyes closed while in his deep meditative state during the reading, he could tell when any of these marks weren't in the right places. Then Aron would suggest that the geologist change the marks, or lines, this way or that, to better identify the areas being referred to.

Later a realtor in Montana requested a reading on Earth changes. He had studied the Edgar Cayce readings, as well as others, and he knew who had given readings on the subject of Earth changes. He wanted to be able to help people move to safer areas, and his questions were based on that premise.

As a result of the readings on Earth changes, we learned some interesting concepts. We'd like to discuss these before getting into some of the details.

For instance, it was given that the vibrations and actions from negative attitudes have not only influenced the environment but also have expanded out into the Universe. Negative energy from those thought-forms boomerang around the solar system and return to affect the Earth in some disaster—the law of cause and effect in operation.

Therefore, we were led to understand that mankind has to take some responsibility for the cause of earthquakes. Also, we caught a glimpse of the possibility that earthquakes don't have to happen because the movement of the tectonic plates and other physical causes can be influenced by our thought-forms.

Mankind, as a whole, has turned his back on his responsibilities toward God. Therefore, destruction and upheaval have come and will continue to come upon the Earth. God is not to be blamed for this. Responsibility for these catastrophic activities lies with humankind because of its negative and destructive attitudes. It is still true and will remain to be that whatsoever we sow we will reap—which is the law of karma. It is not productive to fall into a guilt syndrome over the responsibilities for these things. Rather, be grateful that we are now aware of this and can begin to work in a more united way towards filling our thoughts and actions with love and changing our negative attitudes to positive ones. Earthquakes and other disasters bring our thoughts back to the reality of what is really important in life and thus draw us closer to God.

Because thoughts are seeds, it follows that we are all sowing seeds seven days a week. Our attitudes and motives determine what thoughts we keep in our minds. For the most part, if they are negative or destructive, that is the harvest we will reap; if they are constructive and positive, the crop will be positive. The sowing and reaping go on continually for an individual, a family, a city, a nation, and for the whole world.

When people ask Doris and me when the Earth changes will occur (so they can sell their house two weeks before it happens), we usually encourage them to develop their own intuition and follow that guidance. Nevertheless, we urge everyone to never make decisions or take action on the basis of fear. We also remind them that if we should perish in a disaster, it is only the body that is destroyed, our real selves live on and move on to another realm.

Since it is very difficult to know the day and hour when an earthquake will occur, being prepared is very important so that an escape route can be planned and so that we may consider what responsibility we might have when it occurs. It would be beneficial to live our lives in a way that will prepare us to help those around us. Certainly, those who survive will be needing much help and comfort. Many will need medical care; all will need compassion and comfort.

But beyond that, it has been very difficult for me to pinpoint time from the plane where this information is obtained. On that "other side" there is no difference between the past, present and future. It all exists as now. So if we will prepare ourselves now (spiritually, mentally, physically, emotionally and materially) and focus on the sequence of events that act as a precursor, we will be as ready as it is ever possible to be. You will find the sequence given later.

Further, the information from the readings is not meant to be sensational, nor is it intended to alarm or to cause panic or distress, but since being fore-warned enables us to be fore-armed, it gives us an opportunity to consider whether there is anything we can do about it. Of course, there is always the hope that in turning to God upon being made aware of what could happen, the disaster might be avoided altogether or at least be minimized.

Remember how it was with Jonah when God sent him to warn the city of Nineveh? Jonah told them that in 40 days Nineveh would be destroyed. The ruler of the city knew what they needed to do and proclaimed a fast for everybody, urging them to turn to God in hopes that the city would be spared destruction. As they all did this, the city was spared. Therefore, it could happen in our time as well.

During those days in the '70's, we heard about a wonderful lady by the name of Agnes Sanford, who had been greatly used by God as a healer and teacher. She believed that part of her mission in this life was to pray over the San Andreas fault, so that the damage, which might be caused by any earthquakes along this fault line, would be diminished. Most everyone knew, even then, that scientists had reported that the Los Angeles area was overdue for a major earthquake disaster that could hit the area within 20 to 50 years from then. However, it didn't surprise us a bit that it hadn't come yet. The faithfulness of this devoted woman to her mission had been very powerful and effective.

The last we heard of her was that she had grown elderly and no longer had the strength to stand alone against the San Andreas fault with her prayers, and she was asking for volunteers to take her place. We don't know if the volunteers came forth. She has been gone now for some years.

We have come to believe, however, that when people turn to God and begin to think and live in a Godly fashion, they generate a different set of vibrations around themselves. That, in itself, can change what they draw to themselves.

Though earthquakes and other disturbances are predicted, these destructive effects can be reduced or forestalled through prayer and people making a change in their attitudes and motives by turning with their whole hearts to God. Even if the earthquakes, as indicated by the readings, do take place, keep in mind that it is not the event that is the important aspect. What is of most importance is that one learns from the event. Therefore, though one may encounter difficulties and troubled times, it should be received as a time of opportunity to learn, to grow, and to serve, instead of just a time of catastrophe. Many people have told us that as a result of what they've learned from our and Edgar Cayce's readings on Earth changes, they are praying that our country can avoid them or at least that the damage might be minimized.

The readings tell us that earthquakes are the result of the interaction of the laws of the universe—that is, maintaining a balance between all the asteroids, planets, the orbital shape of the planets about the sun, and other solar systems **and** to the effect of the thought-forms and attitudes produced by humankind. The energy from these interactions with the solar system can release vibrations that can cause these energies to return to Earth and result in earthquakes, tidal waves, and shifting of the poles. All of this would, of course, bring about a severe degree of destruction.

Doris and I hope these Earth changes never take place because of the severe destruction to people, land and buildings. However, should they occur, we must remember that the opportunities for doing what is right have never been greater than the moment in which we are presently living.

Early on, we sincerely believed that the earthquakes described in the readings did not have to take place if people would turn to God. But now we understand that these great changes have to take place. However, if people in any location would stand together in unison, they could diminish the damage to their particular area.

Another event will also take place, which is known as a pole shift or Earth flip. The result of the flip will cause the stars, the sun, and the moon to appear to fall.

When the Earth flips, the entire planet will rotate quite rapidly to a new position. Depending upon where on the planet we observe this change, we will witness something different. If we see this flip at night and it is a clear sky, it will appear as if the stars and the moon are falling. Should we observe this change during daylight with the sun shining from a clear blue sky, it will appear as if the sun is falling. In both cases it is the planet Earth that is moving as it rotates to its new position.

We are happy to see that government officials in danger areas, such as those around Los Angeles and San Francisco, have been making preparations for possible disasters. Church and business leaders have been meeting from time to time to be briefed on possible disasters and have been encouraged to make any possible survival plans they can. The American Red Cross and other civil defense organizations have been working with them on this. Anyone can obtain excellent survival plans from the Red Cross office in any city. Following their suggestions will bring a measure of inner peace.

Scientists interested in earthquake prediction have been studying animal behavior as a sign of an impending earthquake. The information from the readings gives some insight on this method of earthquake prediction.

For instance, the readings say that deer, beaver, and bear are very sensitive to these changes. Smaller animals, such as foxes and squirrels, are good indicators as well. And birds can be very sensitive; swallows and even parakeets will become very restless as an impending disaster approaches. Horses and household pets are known to become very nervous or agitated the day of a major earthquake.

This perception is based on their keen ability to sense minute environmental changes both in the Earth and the atmosphere.

Wildlife will also be sensitive to any disturbances within the Earth; those animals that are very close to the land, close to the Earth, will be feeling very small vibrations for they are very sensitive to these. They will also smell the air. Prior to an earthquake, the ozone content will change, will become more pungent, not to the human being but to the animal. The ozone will increase sharply, come to a peak, stay for a short while at that point and then decrease logarithmically.

The reason for this is because pressure in the atmosphere is increasing; therefore, the ozone content is increasing as some of the layers in the outer atmosphere are coming together in a much denser pressure.

One of the more revolutionary ideas from the readings in earthquake prognostication is the suggestion that there is a temperature increase in the Earth's crust prior to an earthquake. As an earthquake nears, the temperature will start to rise. The more severe the earthquake, the more rapid the temperature rises, and this could be detected as much as 10 to 12 hours in advance.

The temperatures need to be taken at a great depth, however. The deeper the measurement is taken, the more precise are the prediction possibilities.

The land temperature, the Earth's temperature, will increase. Not drastically, not suddenly, but a little at a time until the Earth temperature goes to about one half to one degree above what it normally should be.

When it reaches that value—watch out. You are then approaching a very dangerous condition. By sinking a hole two hundred feet down into the ground, having some sensor and keeping an eye on the temperature within the Earth (it would be better if it were deeper), you would find a much better indication there.

Also, the deeper you go, the readings say, the greater the advance warning of a pending earthquake. For each hundred feet of depth, two or three days can be added to the advance-warning period.

If you sink the hole down to 1,000 feet more, so that you have 1,200 feet, then you have about 20 days prior to anything taking place. So the deeper you go, the more accurate the information will be and the longer warning period.

Another place to look for warnings of impending Earth changes, according to the readings, is to the heavens.

When Mars is in a direct line closest to the Earth and will shine rather brightly and when Uranus will be in about ten to fifteen degrees above the horizon, there will also be a direct line between these two planets to the North Star. The brighter the North Star is shining, the more severe will be the earthquake. The closer it is to the Earth, that means there will be some disturbances, but as it is kept farther away and it is shining very brightly, and Uranus is at a very low altitude above the horizon, there is also a direct line then from it (Uranus) and the planet Mars and the North Star, and there is also a short distance (at the same time) between Uranus and the North Star. Then watch for severe earthquakes.

The brightness of the North Star is an indication, and that brightness will precede the earthquake. So will the angle of declination of Uranus also be an indication. As the angle is lower, then the severity of the earthquake can be increasing.

The information suggests that Uranus is the point of balance between the North Star and Mars. Mars is like the spring. Uranus is the check point and is trying to maintain the balance. This alignment is not the cause of the earthquakes but only an indicator. In other words, Uranus and Mars are not the sources themselves. The sources of these upheavals are the human inhabitants of the Earth and their thought-forms. The readings are consistent in suggesting that humankind has the ability to control the Earth changes. We are the sources of the earthquakes. We are the ones who are influencing the Earth movements by our negative attitudes and thought-forms. These set up vibrations that affect both the Earth and outer space.

One of the more interesting suggestions presented is that when there have been severe earthquakes, there has been a correlating deviation in the orbital path of Mars.

The readings go on to say if one would go back to check the time when Mt. Vesuvius burst forth and Pompeii was buried, a very interesting relationship between Mars, Uranus and the North

Star would be found. The same relationship would be discovered when Mt. Pelee erupted. There are other examples given, such as the 1964 Alaska and 1906 San Francisco earthquakes.

In everyone of these, so has there been a deviation from the path, that is, the orbit of Mars.

When Vesuvius buried Pompeii in 79 A.D., the readings say that the deviation was rather severe. When Etna erupted, it was not nearly as severe. When Pelee, on the island of Martinique, in the West Indies erupted in 1902, the deviation was severe, also. That eruption destroyed the town of St. Pierre and killed approximately 40,000 people.

You can measure this Mars deviation, of course, by distance, by observing the distance where it was the previous, not the previous year, but we measure it by the previous five years, and there will also be a change in the light coming from Mars. In other words, there will be a shift toward red and there'll be a deeper red. There are many ways to measure this deviation, but these are the most obvious ones.

The readings indicate the Earth changes will occur in three phases and over a period of years.

During the first phase, as we approach the next 100 years, the readings foretell many dramatic geographic changes in the years ahead. In the beginning these changes, especially in the United States, will be minor.

The first indication that the major predicted events are about to happen will be the eruption of Mt. Vesuvius and Mt. Pelee. These events will be the second phase.

An eruption of Vesuvius is linked up with Pelee. And that'll cause damage, not only to Italy but also to France, to Norway, to the Scandinavian countries, but in the same time period, you see looking ahead, as one land mass is sinking, another land mass is emerging. So the land mass as a whole, if you are calculating the distribution of land, the ratio of land to the water will be about the same.

Therefore, the first phase will be the eruptions. During that time period as you look ahead there will be the rising and falling of land masses. These events will be followed by a tremendous tidal wave, caused by severe quakes in the seabed that will start in the Indian Ocean. Another tidal wave will also hit Japan; and a third tidal wave will make its mark on the United States with devastating force.

When the catastrophe strikes India, it will cause severe damage before moving north to Japan's coast. *The eastern coast of India will be rather badly damaged, very badly damaged, with the result that there will be some severe inundations taking place.*

The enormous tidal waves and earthquakes will destroy much land in Japan, so much so, the readings say, that Japan will go under.

When we say that Japan will go under, not all will disappear immediately. It will take a little time, a few months or more, and most of the land will disappear. So Japan as we know it now will eventually be a thing of the past. The only land remaining of Japan will be a few scattered islands.

Now, near the coast of China, a land, a small island will start to rise.

The readings predict that earthquakes and inundations will substantially alter the western coast line of the United States. Starting from the southern part of the coastline at the Mexican border, Baja California, Mexico, will be separated from the U.S. It will be an island. Looking up through California, San Diego will disappear and so will San Clemente. Much of the Los Angeles basin will be gone in a deluge. The coastline will move inland from 50 to 100 miles from its present position. Cities east and north of Los Angeles, such as Pomona, Bakersfield, Fresno and Turlock will be the new coastal cities.

Much of the western part will be either gone or only islands remaining here and there. The entire coastal region from San Diego to San Francisco will be full of small islands.

To reach the new sea coast is very treacherous, so there has to be new charting made so the boats can go in safely. There is great activity in rebuilding new sea ports for the economy again to recover. Much has been lost, both in lives and in buildings, as well as in investments.

In San Francisco, much is gone. Sacramento is a seaport, and the coastline goes over to the west and ends up around Eureka. And here it stops.

Moving north toward Canada, British Columbia will be affected but the readings say not to a great extent at the outset. Seattle will be affected but not to a great measure, at least not immediately. The southern part of Washington will be inundated for a few miles.

Oregon from around Roseburg and Eugene will be completely inundated, continuing inland to almost as far as Idaho, leaving most of southern Oregon almost like a peninsula. Southern Oregon will be safe for a period, but then that also will go into the water.

During this period, the eastern seaboard will not escape major change.

The city of New York will have a tremendous amount of devastation. There will be vast fissures, even on the island of Manhattan. Much of that will also be gone. The area known as Long Island will also be affected. For that part will be completely separated from what is known as the mainland, and there will be devastation on the south, east and north coasts of that area known as Long Island.

The part that is now known as the Bowery, where the lower part of Manhattan is, is gone. While the upper part toward Yonkers and toward the upper state of New York has also been touched. It goes as far south as the city of Washington D.C., which has also been touched in a few places. The damage has not been as great here.

Going westward, (from the east coast,) many of the areas around the Great Lakes have fallen into the lakes, so the Great Lakes are even greater now. The St. Lawrence Seaway has been enlarged tremendously, simply because of the breaking away of the soil of the Earth.

So we have a country that is smaller by about three to four hundred miles.

The Canadian border in the northeast will also be affected. Quebec and Ottawa will feel much of it. On the western part, Vancouver, British Columbia, will be damaged but not nearly as much as in California. And there are some very great inundations in British Columbia, which will result in great water inlets. The people of Vancouver will have to move 15 to 20 miles farther inland, as the coast line will be changed.

The readings caution that there will be some very difficult periods for people, financially, physically, and spiritually. It will be difficult for those who do not have a plot of land on which to grow some vegetables for there will be shortages of food. Note this interesting observation during a period of one phase of the Earth changes:

There has been a number of great shortages of potatoes. Potatoes can be a staple product for eating. It contains a number of vitamins which would be useful, particularly in the stressful situations that the people will be subjected to. Many people, the greater part of the population affected, will not have any access to land (for gardening). There will be and there is a very great panic, and this panic is not subdued overnight. By the time these changes are over, many people will have moved inland to Nevada and Arizona.

Many who have studied our Earth change readings have made certain efforts to prepare themselves for these changes. Some in the obvious active earthquake zones have made arrangements to relocate to other parts of the country. Others have felt a mission to remain where they are, so that they might be able to help those around them who survive.

Again, we urge those who ask us, not to make any decision out of fear or panic. When in doubt, do nothing. Pray and consider the matter in a rational state of mind, and then follow whatever guidance is given. Keep in mind that we cannot prepare for every eventuality.

In a reading in the 1990's, the following information for the time that lies ahead was given.

The world as it is now going, is headed for a series of events. The first is the Earth changes with the accompanying pole shift; the next event will be a longing for greater spiritual understanding and growth. So the changes that are about to come to your world, not only in consciousness but also in the Earth structure, will affect everyone. Some of the landmasses will be going into the water while other lands will be rising from the oceans. There will be changes in the educational system, political system, in religious thought, in spiritual growth, in behavior to one degree or another. Changes will be around everyone, so each one can recognize that he or she has a responsibility to carry out and has a contribution to make towards the betterment of the world. Keep in mind not to be afraid. For the changes have a number of contributing factors. First, there is the weakness in the Earth structure. You can expect from this earthquakes, volcanic eruptions, tidal waves, great changes in the weather patterns with a great amount of rainfall in the Midwest. There will be stormy weather in the Southeast, and also the Southwest, as well as in the midranges located near the Gulf, near the water there, like Texas, Louisiana, and other states toward the east.

One can also expect changes in other systems and areas as well. Changes in the language. The language that is used now has deteriorated for many years. But the time will come when this deterioration will stop, and there will be an improvement in the usage of the language. The same goes for the music; the same goes for the behavior of individuals. But also, one can expect that each person has something to contribute. For the world at large is mainly dependent upon what the person contributes.

The environment has suffered because of irresponsibilities by many people. But as the world is seen in your time, so is that a product of the people. People as a whole have all created the world as you see it.

Doris: Lest the people fall under the guilt of the recognition of this, what should they do?

They should recognize that they have the potential to do better. That what they have done has been an act of ignorance, in some cases, stupidity or carelessness, or arrogance in other cases. But the time is coming, very shortly, when people will turn around, not all at the same time, but large segments of the population will turn around to what is better. In that case, the people will begin to create what is good and honorable, and they will create a better world.

Doris: So it is in recognizing it and facing it, and turning from it, and doing something about it and doing it better?

That is correct; that is right. People will take the responsibility when they finally awaken and are startled to see what they have done all these years and for many past centuries. One will have to understand that as they are creating what is better, the responsibility for personal improvement and spiritual growth is still their own.

Doris: Are we to understand that there will be spiritual leaders to help us?

Yes, there will be, to teach you to do right what has been done wrong for so long. But also it is a matter of taking responsibility at the time when it is necessary. For as we said, nothing is automatic. All things require thought, planning, and execution of the plans. But with carelessness, nothing works. One needs to be care-full and kind in order to understand the situation as it is at the present and how it can be improved.

The world, though, presently it is in difficulties, is going through some painful situations, yet the world will go through all this in order to learn. Depending upon how much they have learned from these experiences, when all these changes are over, that will determine how well or how quickly they can turn from their ill doings and do better. For as they learn from the past, they will begin to understand that the same situations cannot go on and that a change has to be made. And that change is the most significant.

If through all the Earth changes, if through all the volcanic eruptions, tidal waves, and changes in the weather patterns, the environment, if through all that, the people can learn, and create a better world, then all this is worth it. For what is better is also on the horizon. What is better for all people is still to come. That is the hope that should be within all people as a whole.

As dramatic as these Earth changes sound, these conditions will seem mild compared to what is just around the corner—within a few years following these events. The readings foretell of the Earth literally rolling over on its side. This phenomenon is labeled axis shift or pole shift, the beginning of another major phase of Earth changes.

(Pole shift occurs when the north and south poles change positions. This results in weather changes, depending upon to what degree the shift would be. This will change the magnetic poles as well as the equatorial line. An axis shift occurs when the whole planet will change its position, so that the continents will face the sun from a different location, i.e. with a 180 degree axis shift [though this is not what we're expecting]. The North American continent would be in the Southern hemisphere, and all the other continents would have their positions changed accordingly).

Chapter 14

Pole Shift: Domestic and World Wide Effect

According to the readings, the cataclysmic Earth changes will take place prior to the shifting of the poles.

The readings say that though the Earth has a precession of about 22.5 degrees from its normal, this precession will increase over a period of time until it no longer can sustain its normal position. Suddenly, the Earth will tilt over about 90 degrees.

One reading describes a scene at the beginning of this event:

Here then we find the axis is beginning to tip. The North Pole will tip in the westerly direction, as the North and South American continents are observed the South (American continent) in the easterly direction. This movement will not be very rapid to start with, but as the axis tips, there will have to be found a point of balance.

Prior to the tip, it will hold itself in a balance of between 20 to 25 degrees for some time. The critical angle is about thirty degrees. At that point, when the Earth starts to tip and depending upon where you are on the planet, the sun will disappear over the horizon, and it will be dark for several days.

So there will be darkness in some sections of the Earth, dusk or light in other places.

According to the readings, the effects of the axis shift will be observed differently in various parts of the world. For example, *Africa will experience a lot of light. China will see the sun as if it were either to rise or fall. For a time the Chinese will not be sure in which direction the sun will come.*

Australia will see something similar. It will be in semi-darkness. In other parts of the world, such as the United States,

107

Norway, the Scandinavian countries it will be dark when the Earth flips.

The wind will be almost deafening, and people will not understand what it is, for they have never experienced anything like this before. The wind will reach speeds of up to 200 miles per hour.

And after the Earth has flipped, within 12 to 24 hours, the new climate will be established.

The readings suggest that mankind should prepare now to record these changes, the wind conditions, the darkness, the light, and correlate them so that they can be preserved for posterity. Then, when and if it happens again, those who come after may not have so much to fear when it again will take place if mankind does not learn.

There will be very little of any Earth changes during the flip itself. There will be whirlpools in the waters off of what was the coast of Southern California. These strange, strong currents will appear like dark circles and will continue for several months until they die out. In the meantime, the waters around what was Southern California will not support much sea life for a while simply because the fish will instinctively not go near that area.

After the pole shift, the third phase of Earth changes will almost immediately take place.

Much of the other countries throughout Europe... have also been devastated. (To repeat) Japan, as we know it no longer is; neither is Hawaii. We see where Hawaii used to be.

The prediction for Japan seems very severe. Even without psychic prognostication, scientists know that Japan lies along an area that marks the rim of the Pacific, referred to as the Ring of Fire, a very seismic active region. It is along this Ring of Fire that the larger percentage of the world's earthquakes take place. Japan experiences thousands of minor earthquakes every year, and it is not unusual for some earthquakes to exceed 6.0 on the Richter Scale.

In other areas, the Arctic and Antarctic regions will find

changes but only as far as the melting of the ice is concerned. All ice on Greenland will eventually melt.

Melting of the polar caps will raise the overall sea level about four feet, the readings say.

The western coastline of the United States will again change dramatically. Instead of land where much of the western states were, there is a great ocean. Here's how the new West coast of the United States will look. Starting at the Canadian border at British Columbia, the coast will go down into south Seattle then cut eastward going straight into Idaho. Southern Oregon will be a thing of the past.

By the way, Crater Lake (Oregon), which is presently on the land, will be a lake within the ocean. It will still be sitting there in the middle of the ocean for some years to come.

Idaho, will be cut in half. The coastline continues into an area around Livingston, Montana. Here, it cuts south wiping off Colorado, Utah, Nevada and California. The inundation covers an area to about Platte, Nebraska. Then it will go about straight south, cutting off part of the Oklahoma and Texas panhandles.

In Texas, the coastline turns west, cutting off much of New Mexico and part of Arizona, returning to the Pacific ocean again, at the position of the U.S. - Mexican border.

Much of the western coast line of Mexico will be affected, and there will not be solid ground between the United States and Mexico. The only way to reach Mexico then will be by either boat or airplane until bridges are built.

In the Midwest and east, parts of the states of Wisconsin, Michigan, Illinois and the other states bordering the Great Lakes will go into the water.

The Chicago vicinity will be inundated. It will be rather a wide inundation, from East Chicago all the way over to Michigan City, Indiana. There will be a very heavy inundation at that point with the result that a river, a very wide river, will open up, and it will go through the countryside all the way down to the Gulf of Mexico with the result that the area known as Lake Michigan will not be completely emptied out, but the water level will be lowered greatly.

There will also be inundations on the western part of the shoreline of Lake Michigan, right around Chicago and north of Chicago. But these inundations will be minor in comparison to that which will take place on the East Chicago area between that area and also Michigan City. One cannot say for sure where the previous lines were, for here we are looking at a very vast area where cities are now under water. And there is a tremendous body of water where land has been. It will be like a delta, then it will narrow down. About fifteen miles farther south, it will narrow into the river, which will be approximately half a mile wide. And it will continue that way until it reaches the Gulf of Mexico. It will go just about due south from Gary, Indiana, all the way down. And though it will curve a little here and there, as we see it, for the most part, it is a straight line.

Other states, such as Maryland and Pennsylvania, will also be inundated.

Instead of being about 3,000 miles across, the United States will be less than 2,000— a loss of about 1,000 miles. Once these new coastlines are established, they will remain that way for a number of years.

The climate in the north will change drastically and abruptly. Instead of severe cold, the climate will be rather balmy. Nebraska and the area around the Arizona coastline will be somewhat mild.

A temperate climate will appear on the western coast more so than on the eastern. However, the humidity on the eastern seaboard will disappear. That cloud bank that holds the humidity will suddenly be gone, and it will be a better climate to live in—comparable to what California is now. Both coasts will be pleasant although the East Coast will be cooler.

As far as the rest of the world, the readings go into some detail and predict major changes in the Earth's geography.

The Aleutian Islands will disappear. Areas around Anchorage, Kodiak and farther north, will be in the water. One benefit to Alaska will be that the temperature, the climate, will be so mild that it will be almost like a veritable paradise.

In addition, land will rise around Alaska to the west (south of the Russian coast line in the BeringSea, and north of the former Aleutian Islands.)

Moving to Europe, there will be some slight changes on the English coast. The western and the eastern coasts will be inundated. The Irish Sea will be wider in some places simply because the coast of Ireland will also be inundated, and land will rise off the western part of England. (Possibly with the rising of the Isle of Man expanding to a larger land mass.)

The other countries will not have too much change, except there will be some severe shaking in the countries such as Turkey and Greece.

Greece will experience a severe earthquake. Italy will blow its top. This is for certain.

The northern part of Europe is quite stable, like Holland, Belgium. France though, will feel the reverberations from the earthquake in Italy.

In Spain there will be land appearing between Spain and Africa, so there will just be a walkway, solid land, closing the Mediterranean.

Later, the area around the Middle East, like Israel, will experience some very severe earthquakes.

Land will be taken away on the eastern part of India for several miles inland and so will the southern tip. The result here will be a land mass appearing in the Sea of India, south of India.

The readings predict strong earthquakes in China that will result in hills and mountains rising and lakes forming in areas west of Peking (Beijing). Fertile places of China will be closer to the present coast and to the south of Peking. We will see a complete change in the agricultural staple, which now is rice. It will change to wheat, and the Chinese people will change their diets to this and other types of food.

China, though it will suffer, will be the first nation that will recover from these drastic changes. The United States will sit for a long time and lick its wounds while China will do something about it (in rebuilding their cities).

In Russia, the land is pretty well solid, but there will be places toward the east coast where faults will become active at that time.

These faults on the eastern part, northeastern part of Russia, will bring certain iundations to the Russian coast itself. When we say inundations, we mean land masses that will be under water for more than three miles inland.

In northern Europe, the Baltic Sea will be larger for a little while until another land mass comes to the surface. The Danish coast will be severely damaged.

Right now it is nothing but islands in Denmark. Large areas of these islands will be gone, causing the strait between Denmark and Norway to be wider. Also, here, a part of the southern area of Norway will be inundated.

Land will rise between north England and south Norway. The English coast will experience difficulties, inasmuch as the areas all the way into London, the southern part of England, the southeastern part of London, and Wales will have gone into the water. But in its place a larger land mass will rise.

The southern tip of South America will be cut away. The western part, up to a few hundred miles, will be inundated. Now, to the west of South America, land will rise, very old land. Very old. It will begin to rise. This is what is known as Mu or Lemuria.

Australia and New Zealand will be spared damage to a large degree. Although, farther north, Indonesia will experience severe damage with the inundations causing loss of lives, and extinct volcanoes will come to life again.

But after these changes, (as given above) the land contours as given here would remain for about two to three thousand years.

The readings say that the Earth's pole shift is not that unusual—it's a natural phenomenon that has occurred time and

112

again. This would go a long way in explaining a lot of geology that still baffles scientists today. But the causes of the Earth's axis shifting is put at the feet of man, the action and thoughts of people, according to the readings:

Here again, the influence, as we mentioned earlier, of the forces about the Earth in conjunction with man's thought-forms, as well as there would also be interplanetary action, such as comets coming by. But these comets come as a result of the thought-forms, and also as a result of the activities of the planet Earth. These thought-forms are, as well, aggravating the collective consciousness of the entire universe.

There was an axis shift in 70,000 B.C. where there was a complete flip, north-south. (Pole shift of 180 degrees.)

There have been minor shifts, five to ten degrees. There has been also a shift in about 200,000 B.C. where there was a 90 degree shift where the north and the south poles were where the equator is.

We also learn that there are many legends in which ancient peoples have noted previous pole shifts and have handed these stories down from generation to generation.

In the anecdotes of the Chinese, the philosophies, and in many of the temples in the Himalayas in Tibet we find accounts of earthquakes and Earth shifts. There have been stories carried down though there haven't been any recently.

At that time, to say that the people were very afraid and bewildered during this earth change period is an understatement. Yet, those who understand what is happening and know that it is not the end of the world can retreat within to their faith in God.

There are signs all around us that these events are coming about and humankind has been given their warnings. In a reading for a strong-willed person who wanted to warn the people in her community about the coming earth changes, this advice was given:

Those who have ears to hear will listen. Those who do not have ears to hear will not listen. It is futile and foolish to try to convince people over and over again. People will only be

convinced as God, Himself, is speaking to them in dreams, in visions, in revelations. That's the only way people will be convinced—or if it actually happens to them.

Your endeavoring to warn people will only frighten the majority of them and for the most part, people will not want to be warned unless they know it of themselves. Unless, they themselves, are convinced. We are not discouraging you; we are endeavoring to give you some wisdom. You may share this with others, but as far as convincing others, it is up to each individual to be convinced. In other words, tell people, but don't force it on them.

In another reading, for a person who wondered what to do in the light of the coming changes, a similar message was given:

God has said, "Before a thing comes to pass, I will tell you of it." I will give you ample warning through many people over a number of years. So nobody is excused. Nobody can say that he has not heard. But if they turn a deaf ear, God will allow them to go through these difficulties. So, therefore, when there is such an abundance of food presently in your country and when you know what is coming, when you can just look on the horizon and see the threats of unrest, disorder, civil strife, and even civil wars, strikes, earthquakes, volcanic activities, economic difficulties, and when one sees all this and still does not prepare as far as food storage and storage of clothing, that in itself is immoral.

Yes, in the aftermath of these earth changes, society will have to readjust to personal hardships and social change. People will have to learn to live in a new kind of world. And for a while, that world will seem to many a hard and cruel place. This was brought out in a reading for a person who wondered what changes, if any, would take place within the society, the culture.

We find that with the changes coming there will be a change in the structure of life, there will be a change in the political world, there will be a change in the economic world, there will be a change in the educational system, there will be a change in the religious system, a complete change from what it is now to that which it will be.

For change itself should not frighten nor scare people. Changes themselves can be very beneficial provided an individual will also look upon these changes as an opportunity to learn, to grow, to serve, and to be of aid to self as well as to others. The changes can be beneficial when the people are prepared, when the people can also look at these changes as another stepping stone in the right direction. But not all people look upon change as an opportunity but rather as difficulties, as problems, as destruction, and in that case so will the changes bring to the individual in direct proportion to that which is held in the mind of the individual. For one needs to consider and remember that like attracts like. Whatever an individual is thinking about, whatever that person is holding in the mind, in the thoughts, that very thing will be manifested in his or her life.

Therefore, the individual needs to understand that with changes, there also needs to be a preparation upon the individual's mind, the physical, the mental, the spiritual, the emotional, as well as the financial. It is this preparation that is so sorely needed among many, many people.

Often, when we are asked to do readings, people ask specific questions about the effects of Earth changes on their particular location. In one reading for a person in Oklahoma, we learned how that area will fare during this difficult period.

As far as the economy, difficulties will be experienced throughout the country. It will be only a matter of degree as to what area will fare better than another in comparison to stability and prosperity. The Oklahoma area will be almost like a bread-basket for many of the surrounding territories and areas.

But that does not mean that one can sit back and do nothing and expect everything to fall into one's lap.

It does mean upheavals, it does mean changes, it does mean some drastic change in the economic market even to the point where many people will have to be re-trained, and many manufacturing facilities will be re-tooling. But, all in all, so will Oklahoma City be a very busy area in years to come, much more than it is now. It will eventually be prosperous but only because people will finally have received the vision to move on and not to just sit back and lick their wounds.

The reading continues by reassuring that the Oklahoma City area will not be touched in regards to tremors and earthquakes, but it will be affected in that many people will run into that city and seek help, shelter, and protection. In one way, the Oklahoma City area will be safe, as far as from destruction by earthquakes, but it will be overrun by people who have fled from the earthquakes in their areas.

Prior to the Earth changes, the climate generally will be getting warmer and warmer, resulting in droughts for long periods. After the Earth changes, and when the coast line comes a little closer to Oklahoma City, the climate will become more temperate. And farmers will be planting a greater variety of crops. Also, when the pole shift has taken place, the climate will be quite temperate.

It is difficult at this time to know exactly where the equator will go, but it will go somewhere east of Oklahoma City. So one will say that Oklahoma City will be somewhat north of the equator. At that point so will the climate be a little more temperate than what it is now, considering all of the changes and considering everything else within the realm of changes.

A young man who was concerned about finding a safe place for himself and his family was given in a reading several areas where he could find safety. But the reading also supplied him with information of the best place for him.

The safest places would be in the southwest such as south of Tucson; in the area of Virginia, in the Northeast, such as in Maine, Vermont, New Hampshire. Other areas would also be in Montana. But the safest place for this individual would be in and near the Tucson area, not too far away from the population. The safest place for all concerned, including this individual, would be a small community, a small settlement, such as up to around 50,000 people, not large cities, not large metropolitan areas. The area near Tucson would be ideal for this individual but as we said, again, don't go too far out into the wilderness—that would be just as dangerous as living in large cities.

Now as the years pass, the events have been taking place more rapidly and with greater intensity, and will continue to do so. For planet Earth is coming into a vortex where all types of occurrences, experiences, and phenomena will take place. The readings assure us that these events are not unusual and that all this has happened before. However, the changes that are about to come are being preceded by events that foretell of these changes.

One has seen these changes in the skies, in the stars. One has seen the changes in numerology, one can see it in tarot, one can see it in the political system. One can see the changes coming about in the economic system. One can see it in one's own personal life, as well as in everything else that is in nature—such as all the chemicals that have been used upon nature itself. This is also a sign of the changes that are coming upon the universe, particularly upon planet Earth.

When we think of Earth changes we should also consider that when there are earthquakes, there should be an accompanying change in people's lives. These changes are meant to be for the advancement of humanity.

For no catastrophe, no difficulty, has been meant to overtake or overcome the human personality but rather to give the individual another challenge, another opportunity to rise above the present circumstances. For one also must remember that the Earth changes that are about to come to your world have been set in motion by the human personalities themselves.

There is always time to minimize such a catastrophic event. There is always time for the changes to be re-directed or postponed. But, in order to do this, humanity will have to change.

117

Doris and I used to believe that there will be either a change within each human personality, an actual earthquake within each individual; or there will be a tremendously large earthquake within the Earth. Now we believe it will be both, not just either/or.

Humanity has decided which way it will be. And in many respects so has the time of no return passed, but there is always time to minimize these changes, to minimize the destructive effect of these changes. But only humanity can effect such a reduction of these earthquakes and upheavals. But it will take the masses to achieve it.

No matter what one says, no matter what one does, no matter what one thinks, the end result will be and must be a change within planet Earth. And, if that change should start on the physical, that is, on the geologic scene, then eventually the change will also come to the human individual. For in all cases, so must there be a harmonious relationship between the human individual and God.

Besides the biblical warnings, Edgar Cayce spoke of the Earth changes that would be occurring, and Nostradamus, in the 16th century, also left quatrains that seem to predict similar events climaxing about the same time.

As far as cataclysmic Earth changes, the readings give us clues for preparation by drawing some parallels for this generation from similar occurrences during the declining years of Atlantis.

Chapter 15

Last Days of Atlantis

O ver the years we have been given much insight into life in Atlantis and other ancient civilizations in glimpses from thousands of readings. We have been able to learn something about Atlantis' social structure, economy, government, education, technology, and medicine. There has also been much given about the destruction of Atlantis by earthquakes and other geological changes, and that aspect is what is important to the challenges facing mankind today.

We find dramatic parallels between that age and our present age. And there is a strong and consistent message that we in this age should learn from the mistakes made by individuals in Atlantis, so mankind in our civilization can avoid a similar fate. In many instances, the same souls that were in Atlantis during those trying days have incarnated again today with an opportunity to correct the mistakes of those past experiences.

The readings have never wavered from a central theme in this matter, and that is that all the devastation and resulting confusion can be avoided if a majority of the individuals, states, and nations would turn toward the love of God rather than pursuing selfish and self-destructive goals.

Throughout your world, there is in many people the fear of earthquakes, the fear of economic collapse, the fear of ignorance, the fear of being controlled by others, and one can go on and on. And many people have spent the energy they have in the wrong direction. Instead of helping to clothe one another with beauty and confidence, many people have been sitting in darkness not knowing what else to do. And so humanity,

119

civilizations, one after the other, has progressed to a point, and then it has started to go backwards or to deteriorate.

One only needs to look at the civilization of Atlantis, how it prospered and how it developed up to a point where the people became slaves to their own technology, and how they allowed their technology and their progress to be their master. That resulted in people wearing themselves out; they destroyed themselves.

The importance of heeding the many warnings and preparing for the times ahead is emphasized by this unfortunate experience which occurred during the sinking of Atlantis.

And so in the lifetime you lived there (Atlantis), so were you warned about the earthquakes, the changes which were to come about. You felt very much though, that your God would protect you so that you would not be hurt or have to go under with the earthquakes. So you really did not take any precautions nor prepare yourself for either moving or making other changes in your lifestyle. You went on as if all things would continue forever and ever. And when the earthquake came, you went under with it, unfortunately. And the soul has always been questioning, "Why did I go under? I trusted in God." But keep also in mind that God sends warnings. God awakens the people so that they can make the changes needed. With every choice made, they will have to take the consequences. So it was in your lifetime in Atlantis.

This person chose to ignore the warning God had sent him.

The following experience shows how a soul's purpose now appears related to his dire experience in Atlantis. He has all the talents and influences needed to fashion a better outcome during this incarnation.

We find also that this individual, being as analytical as we see him here, should begin to understand the planning for the storing of food, the storing of clothing, and to prepare his own mind and spirit for what also is to come. And yet he has all the knowledge that he needs at the present to make the decisions, to prepare others for what is to come on them. For the Earth is

120

now in its final phases prior to the changes, which also are to come, namely the Earth changes, the volcanic activities, the tidal waves and so forth. Therefore, there is no need to fear. Fear will only destroy incentive and the motivation. But it is important now to come and rise to the occasion. It is namely to show forth to yourself what you have become.

His main purpose is now to be an integrator and catalyst among people, both in the field of science, in the field of preparation, in the field of awakening people so that their own consciousness can become alert, and also to understand the season of time and the seasonal changes. Not summer, winter, and so on, but the seasonal changes having to do with both upheavals on the internal, as well as on the external as far as the Earth and humanity are concerned.

Another's experience in Atlantis was more fortunate. During the time before Atlantis' destruction, this person possessed and shared his knowledge that helped others to keep from starving.

You were at that point greatly interested in nature itself, for you had a father at that time who was into agriculture, and he had taught you as a child and as you were growing up, everything that he knew. So it was quite natural for you at that point to also carry it forth, for your interests were, namely, in helping people to understand how to produce more food from the soil.

During a period in Atlantis so was there also a famine. The weather had changed for the worse, and there was a shortage of all types of food, staples, vegetables, and so on. And here you knew about that, that is, your intuition told you. You could look at the conditions, at the situations, and you knew that unless the weather changed there would be a famine. So you started to prepare the people regarding what to do in case the famine should come. And you were very kind about it but firm. You felt the responsibility very keenly, and you did not spare any moments to tell people of what might come. In the beginning, they did not pay any attention to you, but when there came the time where there were shortages, so did they begin to listen. But then it was just a little too late. For it takes a little while before the produce will be bringing forth, that is, before there can be a harvest. And so you tried to tell people how they could produce in their own plot of land where they lived, enough food for them to be able to sustain life.

In still another's experience in Atlantis, we are shown that like today, there was pollution. Some disregarded its effects while others, like this individual, tried to do something about it.

Prior to that life experience, you were now living on the continent of Atlantis during the time prior to the last great earthquake. Your parents were here, you were a female, and you now were a teacher of healing, but you also had become interested in the environment. For the environment in Atlantis at that time was very polluted. In that life experience you started a small group that would try to clean up the environment, not the group itself, but to get some pressure on those who did pollute the environment. You left your nursing profession. You married an individual who was a politician, and the two of you fought for a clean environment, but it was a task that was too great for you, including the group you had formed. And the environment was never cleaned up as it should have been; and you have another opportunity to do the same thing in this present lifetime but now with greater success.

One comparison that should jolt this generation to action is to consider the lack of law and order during the last days of Atlantis when chaos reigned.

The situation in Atlantis, towards its end became very dangerous—just plain anarchy. There was no rule, no effective or responsible government, and no protection for anybody. Each had to protect him/herself as best as was possible.

It might also be comforting to realize that not everyone perished during Atlantis' demise. Many of those who heeded the warnings of the approaching catastrophe escaped to safer areas.

Now prior to that lifetime, you were in Atlantis prior to the last earthquake. You were here a maker of energy crystals, which you also carried with you (that trade) to Egypt where you also went prior to the earthquake taking place. You went with your family to Egypt at that time.

Those same warnings are being given today from a variety of sources, but, for the most part, people are again ignoring them. Some might escape at the last minute, but those who wait too long will find their escape route blocked and impossible.

During the days of Atlantis, there was a tremendous amount of upheaval which had already started earthquakes and tidal waves. There was also a great deal of volcanic activity, but people believed that these would soon die down. When they did not but instead increased both in intensity and frequency, the people became quite concerned. Many tried to sell their property, but they could not even give it away. So many people took what they had and fled the land before it was too late. There were masses of people who did leave the continent, but there were equally as many people, in fact more, who stayed. What happened was that the entire continent started to sink even as a ship would sink, filled with water, and finally it was all over. There was no Atlantis.

Our world, we are told, is fast approaching the point where it will be equal in technology to the civilization in Atlantis. It is at that point where the people have the opportunity to continue to move forward or simply to destroy themselves. If people have not learned from the last experiences in Atlantis, they will repeat their mistakes until one day they will finally learn. But they could save themselves and others a lot of heartache by learning from the past as quickly as possible.

At present it appears that people as a whole have not learned very much. Therefore, the readings urge us to pray and meditate for them, as well as for ourselves. And in the meantime, listen and prepare. Some Atlantean citizens warned others, like this one, about what was to happen to the continent of Atlantis.

Prior to the second earthquake, you started to warn the people about what was about to come. Nobody, or we should say to be more correct, very few, took your advice. It made you quite angry that no more people took your advice. You expected that multitudes would take your advice. But here, people had become lackadaisical, and they believed that nothing would happen, and that Atlantis would continue to exist for centuries upon centuries, and the thing with the earthquake was just something that somebody started in order to attract attention to themselves.

In your present lifetime, so will you have opportunities to warn people not to get into the same attitude again, so as to bring upon themselves the same situations and conditions. Through science, you will have a clear overview of the situations and conditions. Through science, you will have a clear overview of the situations and conditions of the Universe, as well as the individual human being's behavior.

The message seems clear, and the messengers' cries articulate. Whether spanning the centuries since the sinking of Atlantis or from the gentle persuasion of friends and neighbors, we are advised to work toward changing humankind, its attitudes and goals to set its course to the higher plane of God's spirit and love, and, in the meantime, to heed the counsel to pray and prepare.

True, throughout the readings there are warnings of possible devastation through Earth changes. However, the message is not one of despair, but it is one of hope. After the Earth changes and the pole shift, industry will begin to recover. There will be a new surge of hope, a new economy, and a new technology. A newly changed humanity will begin to take over the country and the world.

Chapter 16

The New Century

In the month of April 1994, the beginning of one of our life readings went like this:

As the world as a whole moves toward meeting its destiny, one will discover there is a different kind of energy entering the Earth. This energy was here many ages earlier but left because of dissension because of so many disruptive ideas, greed, and selfishness, which brought about many negative attitudes.

That energy is again trying to enter the planet Earth. Though there is still much dissension among the people, yet there are those who desire to cooperate and endeavor to bring in a different, a better and a new world for all to enjoy. A world of more responsibilities (accepted by each person), but there will be even greater opportunities for all to learn.

It is this energy that will, therefore, revitalize many people. However, it is up to each one to lay hold of that energy. Because it will not come automatically to all people, hoping that they will be instantly changed. Each one will have to work with what is understood to be the truth for the individual at the present. They also need to keep an eye to the future for what is to come. That energy is a comforting energy, revitalizing and healing energy.

There are many aspects to the energy that is coming in. But if too many oppose it, it will not continue but move on. Then it will be a long wait before it will try again.

As we see it now, however, most people will be ready to accept what is to come because of the greater opportunities and the greater understanding among all people. There will come a time on your planet Earth when there will be peace, when there will be love, when there will be cooperation. But that won't come on its own. Instead, it will come as a result of what the people desire to create as their hearts and minds respond to the spiritual promptings.

What you have seen up to now in your world is the product of what the people have created. The people have done that together, unknown to one another; they have all contributed to what you see the world around you exhibits. Just as a disruptive world has been created, the people can also have the capacity to create a very harmonious world. And that is yet to come.

AS HAS BEEN SAID: THE BEST IS YET TO COME

So be patient with what lies ahead. You must be understanding about the changes to come, the difficult events, not only in your country but throughout the whole world. What happens on our planet Earth will affect other planetary systems as well.

Know that you are not the only intelligence in the universe. If that were so, the universe would be in a bad shape. But there are greater intelligences throughout the universe. They are observing the Earth closely, and they are expecting better things to come from planet Earth through the period of the great changes and the coming revitalization.

To go through these changes requires great faith and a greater and deeper understanding of life and a relationship with God. One doesn't come into a higher consciousness just by wishing it so, just by sheer desire. It requires work and dedication.

But the plan is laid out, and it is up to each one to understand the part of the various functions one is to become involved with, as it concerns planet Earth. For a new planet, there must be a new people, a new people who think differently; a people who can live and speak peace to one another; a government who will begin to have second thoughts about how it has behaved and how it has restricted the people to such a degree that they have become paralyzed.

One of the many functions that the government will have is to allow the people to develop themselves, not to harness their energies just for the government's own purposes. They will encourage their development and promote the people, not the government.

These are just a few of the many wonderful events that will take place on your planet. This will take place not only in your own country, but it will also take place throughout the entire Earth. It will be like a great sweep of truth and change for the better in freedom.

Some will feel the effect to a greater degree than others. But all will know that a change has come. There will be some who will not want to participate, some will just watch and be so cautious that they will just look on and by so doing, ruin their own future, their own lives, their own spiritual lives and progress. But there will be many others who will be daring, who will have the courage to forge ahead in freedom.

For the time has come for the preparation of the mind, the intuition, for the stimulus to be injected by enthusiasm, by visions, by planning, and courage through the faith one will have in God.

Much can be done; much more can be said about what is to take place. But what has been said is enough for you to consider what your part will be and where you will fit in. Know that whatever you do to others, the same will be done to you in turn.

The world, as created by God, is a beautiful place in which to live and grow. And when the people begin to take back the authority that they originally possessed and begin to turn from their selfishness to a more understanding attitude, they will begin to help each other instead of intimidating one another. This will be a beautiful time in store for all. But there are no guarantees, of course. One cannot afford to just sit back and wait for it to happen or wait to see if it will happen, and only

then do something. That will never work. One has to take the opportunities as they are presented. People are expected to extend and stretch themselves in order to create a better world.

Wherever two rivers meet, there is turbulence; wherever two oceans meet, there is a disturbance; whenever two people meet who are of different temperament, there's a clash.

Whenever two ages meet, there are upheavals. For example, let us say that the two rivers portray two ages. When they are about to meet and even as they approach each other, the waters begin to be very turbulent and very disturbed. Many who are carried along on these waters may experience distress. They may be frightened because there may be difficulties ahead for all people. But the difficulties are only in proportion to what people perceive to be the truth and how they understand the situation. Just know that eventually the turbulence will ease, and the journey will be more peaceful.

Much has been written and discussed about the consciousness, which is in the birth process now.

A friend of ours, Dr. William H. Kautz, co-author of Channeling: The Intuitive Connection, said it very nicely to us in a letter: "Somehow, what started off as a spiritually motivated altruistic announcement of the dawning of a new 'consciousness,' a birth of a new kind of humanity, has become so bogged down in discussions of the labor pains that the joy and grandeur of the new 'child' is being forgotten."

With all the focus on Earth changes it is important not to lose sight of what it is really all about.

Understand that some kind of earthquake is going to take place. With many of us, it will be an inner quake, sharp enough to allow the highest aspects of our inner selves to rise to the surface and take charge of our lives. Also, for many, there will be a series of geological earthquakes, which will result in severe changes in the surface of the Earth; both will provide an opportunity for all of us to become a new people, better able to productively inhabit the new century. The people who survive this period, though, will undergo many changes within themselves.

This is a wonderful challenge facing us. A wonderful experience. Let us keep in mind this new child to be born out of these changes. We're talking about a whole new people changed to a higher level of thinking, acting, and living because of the changes that have taken place within their beings.

Whichever it is, a quake in us or in the Earth, it will result in the birth of a new people. The new consciousness will endeavor to redeem all the goodness from the past. It will be a blending of the old with the new; it is the replacement of old thinking patterns. It is the replacement of the many old ideas of prejudice and bigotry, which oppose morality. Morality will always remain an activity that will carry with it the greatest of all positive activities of honesty and integrity.

All in all one can look forward to a new hope, a new beginning and a new life. As the new consciousness is approaching, it will have a new impact upon those who have ears with which to hear and eyes with which to see.

The idea of the birth following the labor pains of the Earth changes is a controversial concept. The range of denial spans from total rejection to hedging on the probability. Even those who tend to believe the possibility would like to rationalize destiny. We have heard people say, "Oh, the destruction will not happen. There is so much renewal happening already. So many are turning toward God. To think that the Earth changes are coming is just creating a negative thought-form."

Remember, it would have taken only ten righteous people to forestall the destruction of Sodom and Gomorrah. But more than just two cities are involved now. A whole world is involved. It would take nation after nation of righteous people to forestall the destruction that is predicted.

The view from the Other Side, however, is different. Both negative and positive influences have increased greatly. The increase of the positive has been very encouraging, but much more is needed in order to overcome the negative. There needs to be greater change, and the time is short. There is a need to "work while it is still light, for the night comes when no man can work." False optimism can paralyze as effectively as fear.

And as the present consciousness is passing, the awareness of the new consciousness will be very prominent among most people, but not everybody will acknowledge that another era is upon us. That is the same as turning one's back on the truth or a truth on some particular issue, and believing that if one does not acknowledge that truth, than it will be the same as the truth never existing. Nothing is farther from reality. For whether or not one accepts the truth or ignores it, for that matter, the truth is still there. So it is with the changes that are coming to our world.

The changes are never meant to frighten a people but to let the people understand it is time to recognize another perspective, another attitude, as well as to raise one's own consciousness in one's field of endeavor. It does not matter in what field one is occupied, it matters what one's attitudes are, what one's perspectives are, and how it all expresses itself in one's daily behavior.

The readings give us a glimpse of what life will be like in the era of the new consciousness. There will be major adjustments to be sure, but new methods in technology, such as in medicine and healing, will enhance life greatly.

And as time progresses, so will one begin to see changes coming on quite rapidly in the field of technology, in the field of medicine, in the field of healing. For the original intent of medicine was to heal the people and to do no person harm. And so there will be a movement within the field of medicine throughout your entire world where those who are involved in that field of professionals will begin to recognize the importance of meditation and prayer, so they can pray for one another and pray for their patients. This will be a departure, for the most part, from what it is at the present. But eventually, so will one begin to see that all professionals will be going within more and will be searching from within to find their inner treasures and to explore their own identity.

There will be a combination of the many methods that have already been developed. These may seem to be new methods, except when you say new, "There is nothing new under the sun."

A breakthrough in the healing field will come about by further advancing the use of music and color as therapy. This technique will be much more prominent in this era of consciousness than presently seen and or experienced. This method of healing will be accepted on a large scale by many professionals and institutions. They, together with many healers from all over the world, will teach people how they can heal themselves and thus lead a more productive life.

It will involve more people. It will bring about a better understanding of how the physical body responds to the musical notes, as well as how it responds to the various shades of color. And this is an area that for the present has been explored very little. And people with some insight, people with some fortitude and commitment will be working in these fields. Novices will be the students, but one needs to have intuitive individuals working in such a field so that people can learn to heal themselves. Of course, there is massage, and there is reflexology, acupuncture and acupressure. There is the field of nutrition, and the area of exercise, both physical and spiritual. Spiritual nutrition, for instance, would involve such activities as feedng the soul and spirit by meditation and readng inspirational literature. Altogether, the expansion of various healing methods, if used well and with discernment, will bring a new method of healing for people. But remember "there is nothing new under the sun." It is only new for your present time.

There will be a change in the economy, in as much as more people will have to go back to the soil and begin to cultivate it. This will be a necessity for survival. There will also be a bartering system set up, not by the government but by individuals. People will be struggling under a heavy burden because of the loss of industrial capacity, but they will still try to show to the world that this country is still a great nation.

After the Earth changes, there will not be a return to the former state, individually and collectively. The government will not be able to give help to the many devastated areas. This will make it necessary for the people to stretch themselves, to use their ingenuity and creativity, and contribute to their own survival and success. Because money or loans for the same will be very tight, the people need to have raw material, such as livestock, horses, chickens and other animals so that they can provide for themselves. This will also give them some bartering capacity.

To heat the homes, for most of the generating capacity will be destroyed, there will be a new effort to use the heat from underneath the Earth, known as geothermal energy. This type of heat can be used on a community wide scale. It will take about 20 - 30 years before the economy will return to normal. But it will not be the same as during the former years. People will have learned from the destruction that has taken place and will have realized that it is time to wake up and set up the right priorities for their own spiritual growth and maturity.

The great need will be for jobs. For people do not realize that they have to program themselves into a new economy. There will be more of a bartering system developed and more bargaining for their skills so that they can provide for their needs, not so much for their wants.

There will be many new developments which will come to the surface. Starting with the government, there will be a Department of Peace and a Department of Cooperation. People will no longer be elected to government positions nor sought after just because they are more intelligent than others, or that some are better vote "getters" or fund raisers. But the people will choose their officials on the basis of those who have integrity and honesty, and who possess the capabilities to be a leader. The leaders will be chosen on the basis of how well they have performed as servants. (This does not mean slaves.) A person can only be a good leader if he/she has first served faithfully, loyally, and with honesty and integrity as a servant and then is able to retain those qualities when he/she is in a position of leadership. (In other words, as you rise on the ladder to success, each step of the way, do not forget where you came from.)

The government was never meant to promote itself. The initial role of government was to help protect the nation and its people. This provides freedom for the people to prosper. That role will again be assumed by a new government in the new era of consciousness..

In the area of transportation there will be those who will still use the old mode, like automobiles and airplanes. But a new method will be made available, using the energy from the Earth for the propulsion of all systems. In addition, there will be those who will travel from one part of the world to the other by thought—the ability to transfer one's physical body by thought process from one place to another. This is the mind development that will expand the awareness of one's spiritual capacities as a human being. To have one understand what or who he/she really is will then be the true development of the mind itself.

Communication will be streamlined, to say the least. People will learn to communicate mind to mind. This will be an idea that the telephone companies will oppose.

In the area of education, the task will be to make each person aware that he is a spiritual being, living in a physical body and struggling in a material world. The individual will also be educated to make him aware of his own true identity. This will require some very highly developed teachers, those who will come to planet Earth from outer space to help you. Selfishness will not be tolerated. This will be an important learning process. The new society will try again, and this time it will succeed.

133

Science and technology will have some tremendous advances, but it will require people who have intuitive knowledge and can use it in a practical way. There will be a tremendous advance in the field of healing using rays of light, energy crystals, and gemstones. The scientific community will not be as bigoted then as it is now. Science will be more spiritually-oriented and will consider that the human person is a spiritual being.

In the affairs of human activities, there will be more caring and love for one another, and the words that "you shall love your neighbor as yourself" will begin to dawn on the people. There will still be those who will try to set down dogmas and creeds and (say) that they alone have all the truth. But for the most part so will people learn to work with one another and respect all people.

An interesting aspect of the reading speaks of the manufacture of a type of clothing product that will adapt itself to many different purposes. Such as when worn in a warm climate it will change to a very light substance. When used in a cold climate the fibers will grow to form an insulation. This will be a living product. This will make it possible to use fewer garments as the climate changes from cold to warm and then back to cold.

In addition, the reading has this to say about extraterrestrial visitations:

For when planet Earth stops fighting these futile wars and stops allowing people to starve in one part of the world while food is discarded in other parts of the world, when there is peace in your world, then these teachers will come to visit the Earth. They will come to all who are ready and will be seen by all. They will not look any different than what you appear to be, except that their eyes will have a deep and meaningful light. It is their teaching that you are to look for. The recognition of these teachers, as well as the teaching they bring to you, will be a welcome change of pace for many people.

And in another reading this concept is expanded. Changes will take place, but each individual and people must be prepared to change and move forward.

Each two thousand years your world will go through a change that transforms the consciousness of the individuals, as well as nations, which will improve the perspective each individual, as well as nations. And it will also change the attitudes of the people. However, these changes are not automatic. Just because the change will be present, that does not mean there is a guarantee that everybody will change like a clock advancing in time. But what will be available is the opportunity to change.

But there is new hope projected. And that hope will radiate from within individuals.

The stage has been set now for a breakthrough to replace prejudice, bigotry, and resentment with the love and cooperation of God, and with the unity and with the purpose of God, working of course in all people. But such a thing does not happen overnight. There is a little here and a little there that needs to be changed, a step at a time, in the life of each individual, and when there is peace in one individual, there is peace in that individual's world.

These are exciting times. The transition from one form of consciousness to the next is bound to cause stress and to result in many changes in the life style to which we have become accustomed. Many readings provide suggestions for ways to prepare for this transition.

It is our hope that we will keep in mind that a new consciousness is upon us. How we respond to the new and sometimes difficult situations ahead may very well determine what direction our spiritual paths will take. If we see times that may "try the souls of men," let us hold firmly to the truths we have learned. The transition from the old form of consciousness to the new, may be difficult. But any situation, whether easy or difficult, is merely a learning experience. Situations and experiences from which we learn are only the vehicles to the goals we set.

However, entering a new era of consciousness is only the beginning. There will be a new perception, a new concept coming into the minds of many, many people. But, though this is coming, not all people will be taken up with it. For many there will be who will think and believe differently and firmly oppose such an event as this new consciousness, believing that this is nothing but hearsay, nothing but fantasy.

But the new consciousness is already upon us. It is upon all people. It is important for individuals to recognize that the awareness of the new consciousness will be the factor that enables us to work with it.

From what has been given in the readings, it is possible to pick out many characteristics of this new era. If these are applied now, mankind will be assured of an easier transition through the difficulties.

But the primary step to be taken is a spiritual one, overcoming fear with love and faith. Then, instead of being paralyzed and unable to act, humankind can make that mental leap from knowing that these things are coming, to calmly listing priorities and rearranging finances and changes in lifestyle to adjust to these coming changes.

Keep this in mind: the attitudes that banish fear and build faith are virtues like hopefulness, preparation, purposefulness, love, harmony, cooperation and calmness.

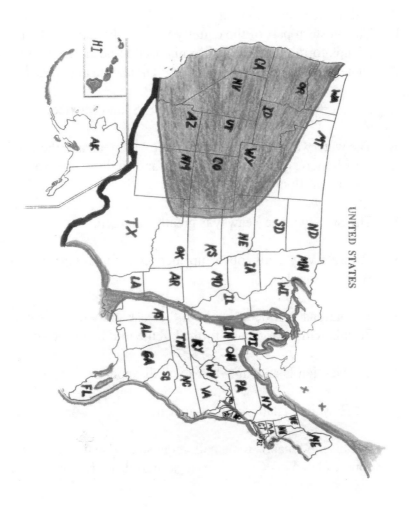

The information for this map was given in a series of readings in 1971 and 1972.

You will notice the following:

1. The western part of the country is severely inundated with islands forming where California used to be. There will be some damage to the panhandles of Oklahoma and Texas

2. A waterway is formed between the U.S. and Mexico.

3. The waterway (rivers) between Lake Michigan and the Gulf of Mexico is greatly enlarged and will cause severe permanent flooding.

4. The St. Lawrence Seaway is greatly enlarged.

5. A waterway will open up between Philadelphia and Washington, D.C.

6. Inundations will occur on both the east and west coasts of Florida with a large lake formed in the middle of the state.

7. The Aleutian Islands in Alaska will disappear.

8. The Hawaiian Islands will disappear.

9. Because the map is too small, it doesn't show the damage done to New York City, Long Island and other East Coast areas.

Tips for Surviving

It is important that you and your family have a plan for survival in case an earthquake takes place. You need to know that in a major disaster of any kind, it may be 72 hours or longer before a rescue team, like the Red Cross and others, will be able to reach you and extend assistance. During that period you have to be able to depend on yourself with the supplies you have stored.

Here are a few items you need to keep on hand

1. Canned and dried foods sufficient for 7 days for each member of your family. If you have a pet, remember they also need to eat. Canned goods have a shelf life of one year so you may need to rotate your food supplies. Remember to keep a non-electric can opener with your canned goods.

2. Water - Store one gallon per person per day.

3. Portable radio with extra batteries be sure to turn it on during the emergency.

4. Flashlight with extra batteries CAUTION: Do not burn candles.

5. First Aid Kit - include any specific medicines needed for any family member.

6. Fire Extinguisher.

7. Adjustable wrench for turning off the gas and water. Be sure that you know where the gas and water meters are located. Also, turn off the main switch at the electric power meter.

8.   A portable stove operated by butane or charcoal. Make sure that there are no gas leaks in your area and that you have good ventilation before turning on the butane stove. Use charcoal stoves only on the outside in a clear area.

9.   Have a designated place where you and your family can meet after the earthquake is over.

Remember: You can't prepare for all eventualities, but what you can do for yourself and your family will give you peace of mind.

During an earthquake: Stay Calm!!!

If you are in your home or office, stand in a doorway or crawl under a desk or table. By all means stay away from windows. Broken glass can be dangerous.

If you are outside, stay away from buildings, trees, telephone and electric wires.

If you are in a car, stay away from underpasses and overpasses. Stop in a <u>SAFE</u> area. *Stay in the car!!!*

After the Earthquake - Check for injuries and provide first aid where needed.

Determine if your area is safe - check for gas, water and sewer breaks.

Determine what, if any, damage is sustained in your home and be prepared for after-shocks. If your home is badly damaged leave it and *<u>do not</u>* re-enter it. Clean up dangerous spills

After an earthquake always wear shoes wherever you walk.
Turn on radio and listen for instructions from public safety agencies.

Do not use the telephone until all is clear.

For further information, please contact your local Red Cross office or your local office of Emergency Management.

About the Authors:
Aron & Doris
Abrahamsen

Aron Abrahamsen, a native of Norway, is by education an Electrical Engineer, having received his BS degree from California Polytechnic State University, San Luis Obispo, California. During his twenty year career in the engineering field, he was at one time a member of a scientific study team to determine the feasibility of sending a manned expedition to the moon with a safe return to the Earth. The result of this study paved the way for the Apollo Program. As an engineer he authored several technical papers, lectured frequently on the Space Program and has appeared on TV and Radio talk shows about his psychic work. .

Early in his engineering career he had a very meaningful spiritual experience with Christ, which changed his outlook, goals, and purpose in life. After many years of study in the Scriptures, and through prayer and meditation, he came into the knowledge of reincarnation and karma. He also discovered that he could leave his body and travel to the Akashic Records where he could obtain information that would be helpful to people. While still in the aerospace industry, he started to give life readings on a very limited scale. This opened up new and meaningful avenues of service. For 25 years he and Doris dedicated themselves to do life readings for people from all over the world. He retired in 1995 because of health problems. Since that time, the tapes & and all the records of those for whom the readings were done have been destroyed by a commercial shredder, mainly to protect their identity & privacy. Therefore, Aron no longer gives life readings.

His work has been written about in such books as Dr. Jeffrey Goodman's *We Are the Earthquake Generation* and *Psychic Archaeology*; John White's *Pole Shift*; Dr. Laile Bartlett's Psi Trek; Dr. William Kautz and Melanie Branon's *Channeling: The Intuitive Connection*, as well as other publications in Japan and Europe.

Together with his wife, Doris, they have conducted seminars, conferences and workshops on spiritual growth, earth changes and dreams in this country and Canada. For over two years they were on the speaking circuit for the Association for Research and Enlightenment on the topic "Be Your Own Psychic." In the winter of 1993 his first book, an autobiography, "On Wings of Spirit" was published by A R E Press. His second book "Holiday in Heaven" published by Ozark Mountain. Publishing.

Doris has over 30 years experience in counseling and is well known for her expertise on the subject of Sound Dynamics, Healing of Memories and meditation. She has conducted classes and workshops on these subjects for many years.

Other Books Published
by
Ozark Mountain Publishing, Inc.

Continue for more books by Ozark Mountain Publishing, Inc.

For more information about any of the above titles, soon to be released titles, or other items in our catalog, write or visit our website:

OZARK
MOUNTAIN
PUBLISHING
PO Box 754
Huntsville, AR 72740
www.ozarkmt.com
1-800-935-0045/479-738-2348
Wholesale Inquiries Welcome